The Maiden of Nazareth

English edition published by Scepter Publishers, Inc., copyright © 2015
info@scepterpublishers.org
www.scepterpublishers.org
800-322-8773
New York

Cover design by Carol Cates
Text design by Rose Design
ISBN: 978-1-59417-241-0
Printed in the United States of America

The Maiden of Nazareth

A STORY OF THE
BLESSED VIRGIN MARY

Javier Suárez-Guanes

 Scepter

We don't know if it happened thus, but it might have.

❖ ❖ ❖

If there is anything worthy in this book,
I owe it to
St. Josemaría Escrivá
from whom I learned to love my Mother the Virgin,
whom he now contemplates in heaven
after having loved her so much here on earth.

❖ ❖ ❖

Contents

About the Author vii

Introduction ix

1 The Lovely Star 1

2 Serene Hope 21

3 The Shade Tree 41

4 A Light in the Darkness 53

5 The Wind in the Crevices 62

6 The Rainbow 71

7 The Footprints of God 78

8 A Diamond in the Sand 89

9 Human Love, Divine Love 104

10 Roadless Horizon 139

11 Time of Love, Time of Suffering 154

12 A Bright Star in the Night 175

About the Author

JAVIER SUÁREZ-GUANES WAS BORN in Madrid. He is of Asturian origin and Castilian heart. After receiving a degree in law from the *Universidad Complutense* of Madrid, he received a doctorate in Rome in 1956. Following ordination as a priest, he went to Mexico to do priestly work in rural areas. In 1962 he went to Guatemala to work with students and members of a youth club.

Next came seven years in El Salvador in another student residence. Upon his return to Guatemala, where he lives today, he became chaplain of the church *Nuestra Señora de la Paz* (Our Lady of Peace). There he wrote this book in his free time. He has also published *Respuestas de la Virgen* (Answers of the Virgin).

INTRODUCTION

I HAD THE IDEA OF WRITING THESE pages while meditating on the words of St. Josemaría Escrivá: "When you love someone, you want to know all about his life and character, so as to become like him. That is why we have to meditate on the life of Jesus, from his birth in a stable right up to his death and resurrection . . . for we do need to know it well, to have it in our hearts and minds, so that at any time, without any book, we can close our eyes and contemplate his life, watching it like a movie" (*Christ Is Passing By*, n. 107).

These lines weren't written as a treatise on Mariology, nor as a life of Mary enriched with historical facts, nor with exegetical or traditional assumptions. It is a story about the life of Mary and her family in Nazareth, the fruit of many years of contemplating the life of the Virgin, Our Lady. Therefore, I have not strained to compose this account. I have merely allowed it to flow as in prayer.

I have had the audacity to delve into the internal and external expressions of Mary and her family and articulate them in the language of today. May she look upon me with mercy and pardon me as she would a child.

I have looked at many writings, but they have not served me well. They either expand or comment on the evangelical texts or fantasize events and personalities that depart from the framework of my story. From the start, I said I wanted—daringly—to apply the spirituality that St. Josemaría Escrivá de Balaguer brought to the world: the sanctification of the ordinary, of work, of everyday existence, a story of the life of the most loved of persons—Jesus, Mary, and Joseph.

I have tried to write as their contemporary, narrating what he saw and meditated upon in those days, not as one analyzing events in the light of historical perspective, tradition, or contemporary Christian asceticism.

It is hoped that these thoughts will serve to introduce the reader anew into those familiar scenes, inspiring prayer and increasing love for Jesus, Mary, and Joseph.

The small donkey of the Holy Family whose story is told, and whose "thoughts" are expressed, could represent any of us (who wouldn't want to have been in his place!).

Confronted by a mindset anxious to depict the Virgin as very, very young, out of fear of St. Joseph's chaste love, I imagine Mary to have been a young maiden in full bloom when she married.

I have placed Mary in the Temple, but not as if she were in a cloister isolated from worldly dangers. There is a tradition that speaks of her as being presented in the Temple at the age of three, but it does not say she remained there to live.

The personalities have been roughly sketched, without exhaustive detail, so that the reader, with his or own imagination, can fill in the gap by personal reflection.

The historical facts, the traditions, the opinions common to authors who have written about the Virgin, as well as the descriptions of the environment, the countryside, and the distances covered, are drawn from *The Life of the Virgin Mary* by Gabriel M. Roschini, O.S.M., who has made a complete study of many writings about Our Mother the Virgin and provides an ample bibliography.

1

The Lovely Star

THE WIND WHIPS THE WINDOWS mercilessly; as a tardy passer-by walks along the street, his clothing blown about as he clutches his mantle. Sheep are bleating nearby; the lamplight flickers, making moving shadows on the walls. Joachim leans his elbows on a rustic table on which he has just studied the accounts, supporting his gray head with his hands. He is heavy-hearted. He reflects, "So much work! And for what?" The son so eagerly desired since his early days of marriage never comes, while he and his wife only grow older.

Ana works in silence in the faint light from the hearth; her lips move silently. Is it prayer? Her gray hairs are arranged in an attractive bun. . . . She was so beautiful when they were married! Hopes blow away like the wind howling in the street.

But Joachim is a man of faith; that he will never lose. He takes up a thick roll of the Sacred Scriptures and sits beside his wife.

"Ana, shall we say our night prayers?"

She looks at him—her blue eyes are still beautiful despite the fine lines on her olive skin—and she agrees. Joachim opens the scroll to Psalm 21, he reads in a deliberate tone:

"My God, my God, why hast thou forsaken me? Why art thou so far from helping me, from the words of my groaning? O my God, I cry by day, but thou dost not answer; and by night, but find no rest."

And he ends: "Posterity shall serve him; men shall tell of the Lord to the coming generation, and proclaim his deliverance to a people yet unborn, that he has wrought it."

His voice breaks; he retires to his room. Ana picks up her sewing, tends the fireplace, and puts out the lanterns before following him into their quarters.

Winter passes; life goes on. At the beginning of spring, Ana feels strange, nauseous. A suspicion starts to flicker in her heart, but she doesn't want to arouse false hopes: she decides to talk to a midwife. . . . Her face lights up with laughter, and her eyes fill with tears: God has had mercy on her: she is expecting a child!

That afternoon she tells Joachim, who is filled with great joy and goes immediately to the Temple to offer thanksgiving to God.

Ana waits a couple of months to tell the news to relatives and friends, all of whom show their joy; some look at her curiously and half-incredulously. Before the end of summer, Joachim gives a banquet so that the news may reach everyone—those at the Temple, the sheepherders, and even the beggars who mill around the Probatic pool.

Ana is happy with the profound happiness of one who knows herself to be fulfilling the will of God. Her time is taken up making baby clothes, and her relatives and friends are always at her side. The small abode is full of joy, like that of many years ago, when they first arrived at this house next to the Temple that adjoins the Sheep Gate where Joachim is administrator.

Summer is spent, and soon autumn comes, balmy and serene. Ana walks awkwardly. Jokingly, she says she feels like Sarah, Abraham's wife, but is quick in spirit to laugh, to share every small happening, or to allow Joachim to show his affection with a gentle kiss, while he says to her: "Don't move, I'll get it. . . ."

Joachim is a pious and good husband, and a wise merchant: prudent in dealing with customers—be they rough or sly—who come with their sheep for the Temple. Skillful at judging the good, he speaks to them calmly and, whenever necessary, shows a certain wry and witty disdain. He is calm and patient, more introspective than talkative. He loves Ana deeply. She, in turn, possesses a more practical and lively temperament that he calms during small domestic contradictions, causing her to end up smiling.

An enthusiastic gatherer of rolls of ancient Sacred Scripture, he hums as he works over them on feast days, hour after hour, even forgetting to eat.

He has gone through difficult moments. He has had to resist the intrigues of some who would have taken away his job, much sought after by those who desired to fill their pockets by means of it. Only his love and fidelity toward Ana prevented him from repudiating her in order to have children with another woman.

The contractions begin the afternoon of a serene day. The midwives come hurriedly, as do some relatives. Fires are lit in the braziers along the corridors and rooms, meals are prepared . . . and the waiting begins. Together with friends, Joachim makes himself comfortable next to the hearth; at times quiet; at times speaking aloud.

"Lord, this child, what will it be? Thou desires something for it; Thou hast given it to us in a miraculous manner, show us Thy will; protect Ana, who is no longer youthful, may they both live, Lord!"

Before daybreak, while the morning star still shines, a midwife comes out for more hot water; loud whimpers are heard. . . . Joachim and the men refill the lanterns, deadened from the long night. There is a brief silence; then, the wail of a newborn. . . . Joachim waits, tensely. The door opens, the midwife signals for him to enter. Ana lies there pale yet smiling. She presents him with a beautiful baby girl whom she is cradling in her lap.

"Oh, Ana, how precious! She will be named Mary, 'the loved one of God,' like the sister of Moses: God bless you."

Months go by; the little one grows before their eyes, healthy and strong, daily more beautiful. Joachim is happy holding her in his lap, enjoying the way she looks at him, while Ana busies herself with household chores. Then Uncle Ben shows up. He is made welcome. He is beside himself with care for Mary. Furthermore, discreetly and efficiently, Ben helps with tasks around the house and in the fields during the summer.

Those are happy years. As soon as she can stand up, little Mary likes to hold on to the sides of the crib, jumping and prattling when someone comes in to look at her. At the age when most children learn to do so, she begins to walk, going back and forth from the arms of Ana to Joachim, laughing delightedly.

Ana is the same as ever, but with renewed vigor. Her daughter has rejuvenated her: capable, active, enterprising, big-hearted with everyone, especially those who formerly served in her home but left in search of a better life that never materialized. Every week she helps some of those who wait patiently on the nearby benches outside the entrance. Thrifty, but not miserly, she makes good use of everything and wastes nothing; a woman of lineage, she conducts her simple life with stateliness; endeavors to dress well—always clean—and arranges herself with care for a feast or when she expects guests. She likes to sing while she works, as does Joachim. . . . Neither knows which of them picked up the habit from the other.

◆ ◆ ◆

Before she is three, Mary is taken to the Temple. She grows very thoughtful at seeing the coming and going of so many people. Joachim lifts her in his arms to see the sheep, and she is fascinated by them, especially the newborn lambs which allow her to pet them and eagerly lick her hand.

Now she begins to learn many passages of Sacred Scripture, repeated over and over by Ana until Mary knows them. Unlike other children, she does not forget them later.

Other times, Mary sits next to Joachim or on his knees as he explains the meaning of those writings.

Some festival days they walk around Jerusalem. The little one marvels at the palaces, the huge walls, the street vendors with their loud shouts, and the occasional passing of mounted cavalry, breastplates and lances glistening in the sun. Sometimes they go as far as the Mount of Olives. Under a large, luxuriant tree, they have lunch while contemplating the Holy City spread before them.

On one occasion when Mary is six, returning from a visit to relatives, they find the streets jammed with an agitated, shouting mob. Joachim picks her up and seeks to evade the tumult but cannot. This is the crowd accompanying a man on his way to be crucified amid shouts, shoves, and hard blows from lances. Bleeding, the man collapses beneath the cross he is carrying. Overwhelmed and tearful, Mary watches.

"Daddy, where are they taking him? Why are they hitting him?"

That summer they visit Nazareth for the first time. Barely able to contain herself for joy, Mary takes turns riding on Joachim's mount and then on Uncle Ben's, asking about everything, laughing, looking about excitedly—at the road where a lizard has just scooted across, then up at the sky where swift swallows or flocks of ringdoves fly.

In Nazareth she has a room to herself, with a large bed and a small window looking out over the valley. At daybreak a goldfinch sings and sings in the orchard while Mary says her prayers and looks at the distant mountains outlined against the red dawn. Every day is an adventure made up of little events. Her cousins and other girls come to play with her. They go into the field with Uncle Ben and to the plantations with Joachim, and in the afternoons she does needlework with Ana and the other women of the house. Then night prayers and bed, tired and content, in a bedroom filled with the aroma of thyme from a little bunch that Uncle Ben had placed there for her in the morning.

What a wonderful time she has in that small hamlet! Clean air, blue sky, flowers, cicadas that sing at noon, birds. She enjoys everything because she loves all the goodness that comes from the hand of God. With Ana she visits relatives. She goes to the river with Uncle Ben. She goes by herself to the orchard or to the chicken coop, where a broody hen rises up with her chicks and red-eyed rabbits munch thistles gathered along the road the day before.

At mid-afternoon they get together in her house or at some neighbor's to play with friends and relatives. Simple games played by modest, happy girls who have no need of greater things to be entertained. Games of long steps and fast turns over tiles; of increasingly more rapid patty-cake; of jumps to the rhythm of a rope; buying and selling; dodging and running away; rolling knucklebones in unerring throws; quickness of wit so as not to forfeit a token; relay races; and monotonous sing-songs or happy dances.

When summer is over, the first rains fall. Preparations for the return journey begin. Regret at having to leave is lessened by anticipation of going home and seeing friends who had remained behind.

◆ ◆ ◆

When Mary has reached the age of reason, her parents present her at the Temple. A benevolent, elderly priest receives her and is very impressed when she responds to his questions without hesitation, simply and with assurance. He introduces her to other women and girls and tells her she may come the following day to stay. She will learn to sew, iron, care for the priestly ornaments, and clean the Temple. In the evening her parents can come for her, since they live so near.

The next day, she is taken early to the small door where other girls and women wait. Some of the girls are her age, some older. Upon entering with them, Ana turns around, and a tear runs down her cheek. She covers herself with a shawl so as not to be seen crying, while Joachim serenely takes her by the arm. In the late afternoon, her parents return and she runs joyfully into their open arms. In the evenings, Mary tells them about all the things she is learning: classes in the Torah, sewing, embroidering, and cleaning the objects for the service.

Starting very young, Mary disciplines her life to the rhythms of work, monotonous study, fulfillment of duty, attention to detail. When it is her turn to clean the sacred place, she takes the opportunity to pray, a silent and intense prayer in that place where she feels the presence of God so close.

One day, she comes out to the Atrium of the Temple with other companions. It is a busy hour with much movement, the bustle of pilgrims, shouts of money changers and sellers, a varied, picturesque throng: peasants as well as Temple merchants, all busy coming and going. Suddenly there are loud voices and screams. Curious people rush to form circles around men who are fighting. Knives are drawn—the peace officers fail to arrive—they attack one another. . . . A young man is left lying on the pavement, blood gushing from his chest, while another flees and loses himself in the crowd.

A young woman kneels over the wounded one. Shouting his name several times, she desperately hugs him, staining her face with his blood. Mary, next to her, stares at her, terrified; some women pull her away. The lamenting and sobbing of the young woman over the corpse can still be heard. Mary lives her first experience of death. Seeking refuge in the arms of Ana that evening, she tells her what happened, then asks:

"Why, Mother, why do they kill each other?"

"For ages we women have asked ourselves this question, oh how many times, my daughter! How valuable a life is! So much care lavished on it from childbirth! And in an instant, either from vanity or for revenge, it is destroyed."

"Yes, Mother . . . I want always to be meek."

Mary learns to read and recite the Psalms that are part of her faith to give glory to God. Joachim listens to her with growing wonder and immense joy. Ana gives her a penetrating look, searching for the inmost depths of her daughter: *What does God want of this girl? Because his Spirit is with her.*

The faithful servant who has been with Ana since she married cannot understand how her "little one" knows all these things. On days Mary does not go to the Temple and stays at home, the servant patiently teaches her to cook what the good woman has learned during the many—at times monotonous—years of sorrow and joy, in good times and in bad. Simple stews, savory dishes flavored with the special seasoning that affection supplies. These are the well-tested formulas used by the women of Israel for centuries—Sarah had already prepared these same stews for Yahweh. Mary learns to keep the hearth just right, to clean the cooking utensils, to place the newly bought food in a fresh place—where air flows—well away from the obstinate cat.

Ana—hair pulled back and wearing her smock—makes bread the day before Friday. Mary observes how she kneads the bread with her sleeves rolled up; strong, delicate, turning and pummeling the dough over and over, until it is well mixed with the yeast within. Well covered, it spends the night "growing" until the next morning, when her quick fingers form the dough into small buns. Placed on a long wooden palette, the buns are put the oven which Joachim lights quickly when it is full. It is an old oven, clean and sparkling, that has served many generations and which Uncle Ben restored carefully when they came to live in this house. Some psalms are recited, the smoke clears, and Mary hops with impatience as she waits for the small bun that Ana always makes for her with her initial on it.

Studying, working, games, prayers, outings, shopping with Ana and the servant on market days, visits to relatives, friends; days and nights go by, seasons glide, and years melt away in the grace of God. Little trials: a broken nail, a lost toy, a friend who teases her. And simple joys: the first bunch of cherries that Uncle Ben brings, newly born kittens that try to climb out of their basket, a little chick that eats out of her hand, a costume jewelry necklace that Joachim brings her after being away for several days, cloth for a new dress that Ana buys. . . . The dreams and realities of everyday life mingle: a small chore to be done, tears shed for a friend who moves away, joy at the announcement of the next trip to Nazareth.

❖ ❖ ❖

Years come and go; so do summers and winters, human loves and hatreds and ambitions. One night there is a commotion: shouting, running, fires, and uncertainty; panic in the faces of those who are being pursued and finally apprehended; mounted soldiers and horsemen thunder on the uneven cobblestones. No one goes out at night; there is fear in their eyes. Not a light is on, and no fire burns in any hearth.

They have all slept badly, huddled in a back room. At daybreak they hear pounding at the door, voices commanding them to open; the shouts increase. Before it is broken down, Joachim, wrapped in his poncho, opens it. Soldiers burst in, pushing him toward a corner with their staves. A frightened Mary, already awake, looks on with her big, sleep-bereft eyes; the servant sobs.

"Anybody here? Anyone hiding?"

They search violently, ripping curtains, damaging furniture, smashing utensils, all the while heaping insults on fugitives. An officer surveys the group: hard, contemptuous. Ana presses Mary to her breast while hardly raising her eyes, observes Joachim, who unflinchingly holds the officer's gaze. She whispers to Mary: "Pray, my daughter, so that they don't take your father, he is not involved in anything, but the justice of men is so unfair! Oh! God, do not abandon us!"

"If you are hiding anybody, you will pay for it with your lives!"

They leave, with the same belligerence with which they entered. Ana gets up and begins to put the house in order. From the floor, Mary picks up a little clay bird brought to her yesterday, now broken.

Several days go by before she returns to the Temple with the other girls. Some don't come back: Their fathers were involved in the insurrection.

The chores, the cleaning, the classes of Sacred Scripture—all neatly scheduled; these are the weave and weft of Mary's learning. Sheltered by the Temple and the good example of her parents, her soul opens like a precious flower to the love of God that she carries within.

The child Mary brims with piety when saying her prayers, singing the psalms and reciting the passages of Sacred Scripture that Joachim selects from among those she has learned that day. Her soul rises toward God, free from the bonds of the flesh, and pierces her spirit with pure joy; at the same time, she remains a little girl like her companions, with feelings that overflow in laughter and at times in tears.

Ana observes her thoughtfully. *What does God want from this so singular daughter of mine? Her soul grows in beauty as does the beauty of her countenance and the grace of her carriage.*

Many times, it is Joachim who goes to fetch her at the Temple. With his venerable white beard, his measured gait, and his forthright gaze, his stateliness clears a path for him among strangers and acquaintances. He explains to his daughter the details of this noble building, the ancient Jewish customs, and the heroic stories of his people in defense of their faith.

On days when their walks are longer, they observe the city from the skirts of a small hill they call Golgotha. Joachim knows Jerusalem well: its history, its buildings, its narrow streets, its neighborhoods—be they crowded or grand—and its people as well: Palestinians or foreigners whom they come across on their walks and can identify from their dress or accent. Even though he is not a man of great means, he is an almsgiver, always carrying in his bag some coins that he gladly gives to Mary, aware of the grateful looks of the poor who swarm in the city.

Mary has a special predilection for a blind boy who sits daily under the shelter of the Door of the Sheep with his begging bowl in hand. He sings or recites verses about the kings of Israel, its heroes, the Messiah to come, the one who is near. . . . Joachim and Mary, surrounded by other onlookers, listen with pleasure.

"Father, why does he talk so much about the Messiah? Is it that His coming is near?"

"I can't tell daughter, it is difficult to know when the fullness of time will be: I have meditated much about Him and believe that the time of His coming is nigh, but I couldn't tell you when and where."

"His mother will be a virgin and very beautiful, right, Father?"

"Yes, daughter, lovely like you . . ."

His daughter looks at him thoughtfully and blushes. Mary takes food to the blind boy—he knows her name because her friends have repeated it when seeing her helping him.

"Why do you sing so much to the Messiah?"

"Because he will come soon, he will heal my eyes, and I will see the light, the trees, the faces of the people, and yours, Mary. How I yearn for God to grant me sight to see him! Because I know people by the sound of their voices, and you God loves immensely."

One bitter autumn afternoon, before they sit down to supper, they smell smoke, an intense, acrid reek. Ana goes to the door and sees flames in the neighboring house.

"Joachim . . . fire!"

Everyone gets up to look. The flames grow; the frightened dwellers rush out carrying bundles to the street; they call to each other with loud shouts. Curious neighbors gather, their tragic faces lit up by the flames against which they raise their arms protectively. Together with Uncle Ben, Joachim and other neighbors go up to the roof. The women fill buckets with water that are passed from hand to hand and up the wobbly ladder. The smoke makes them cough—there are gusts of wind which bring the fire closer and others that blow it away. More of the curious approach to look on excitedly from the street, muttering. Joachim's face is red, is hands are blackened, his eyes tearful. Mary, at age eleven, does not tire from carrying water. The flames reach her bedroom; clothes and furniture catch fire. From the door frame she sees them burning and shudders. How many small, cherished things disappear forever: clothes, once-begun projects and handiwork, the antique chest, a small doll . . . !

"Oh, my God! May only my room burn, protect the rest of the house!"

The wind changes, the flames veer, the remaining flames are put out. The danger is over.

Ana wipes the sweat from her face with her sleeve; Joachim comes down the ladder. Mary comes to him and seeks comfort in his arms, crying quietly while she looks at her wet and blackened room.

"Don't cry, my little one, we are all well. Let's give thanks to God who has saved us. Tonight you will sleep with us." And he gives her a kiss that calms her sobbing.

◆ ◆ ◆

Mary grows, gradually becoming a woman. She leaves the studies in the Temple and stays at home to help with domestic tasks. Her light eyes are as though the sky had mingled in them; her hair is long and unbound, the color of ripe wheat. There is spring in her stride, her speech is measured, her skin so slightly olive; her neck slender, her hands fine and strong. Her gaze is pleasing, as is the tilt of her mouth when she laughs.

Ana teaches her how to cook special dishes, how to make bread, how to wash fine cloth, and how to take care of flowers. She even is taught how to look after the small cantor bird, given to her after the fire, which upon the first light of dawn makes the mornings joyful with its song.

In the afternoons, when they cannot get ready-made thread, they spin it on the spindle or weave on a small loom that Joachim bought for Ana before their daughter had even been born. Mary learns rapidly, and her work is perfect as soon as her hands become used to it: with them she moves the shuttle in time to rapid movements of her feet that open and close the warp.

Other young women and relatives come to learn under the tutelage of Ana, serious at times, and merry for the rest. Other days, they embroider or sew. Mary does this to perfection. Before starting work she offers it to God. She helps the rest with their doubts, without vainglory. Skillfully she threads the coarse needle and pierces the cloth with an accurate stitch pushed on its way by a small silver thimble, a present from Ana. When finished, she leaves her work folded, threads gathered in a big ball.

As evening approaches, they pray together until Joachim returns from work.

Months and seasons and years go by in monotonous sequence, full of small happenings and things done daily with ever more love. Mary never goes out by herself. She is becoming an extremely beautiful woman, slim and modest, always impeccable and well-groomed; when she goes out, she covers most of her face with a veil. But it is hard to hide a star. Some young men prowl around the house; Ana becomes concerned, as the times are uncertain. The powerful go about satisfying their greed or base appetites with impunity.

In those years, despite differences in personalities, attitudes, and status, Mary has become very close to a young woman somewhat older than she. Mary helped her in spite of the teasing of other friends and the exigencies of her parents. The affection was mutual, fueled by the great admiration the friend felt for Mary. They worked together, read together, and together shared their friendship with other young women.

Her friend would frequently spend the afternoons with Mary, and she in turn went to her house, a big home, conveniently located not far from the Temple, with a big formal room on the top floor where, at Passover, their families celebrated the ritual supper together.

Upon growing up, the friend became beautiful and self-indulgent, with no enthusiasm for anything, for her parents had already promised her in marriage to Marcos, a man of experience, a wealthy merchant. Mary encourages her not to lose her eagerness for work, for tasks proper to home, for things newly learned or yet to be discovered; the other listens to everything amiably, but begins to talk about her necklaces, her dresses, the color of her nails, her boredom. Still, the friendship continues because they are fond of each other. Mary turns to God, prays for her friend, and tries to think how to draw her out of her egotism and make her interested in others.

One afternoon they see some lepers walking toward the outskirts of the city. They follow them for a distance and see their wretched dwelling. They decide to take them clothes and food. Mary tells Ana, who has her doubts and speaks to Joachim. "Woman, she is no longer a girl; it is a good deed she has in mind. They can go with Ben."

And her friend becomes enthusiastic about something besides herself and her own things. She obtains clothes from among her relatives and friends, they gather foodstuffs and money, then happily they take everything to those poor people despised by society, who are at first wary, then thankful.

Mary is especially moved by a little boy who always receives them with immense joy, staring at them with huge eyes from a face deformed by the illness.

"Mary, will you teach me to pray?"

And little by little Mary repeats brief prayers with him.

"If I always pray to God, will he cure me?"

"God loves you very, very much, and he will give you the best."

"My grandfather says the Messiah will come soon, and he will heal me. Do you believe that, Mary?"

"The Messiah will be very good, especially with children who pray. Come, give me your hand and repeat after me: 'I love the Lord, because he has heard my voice and my supplications. Because he inclined his ear to me; therefore, I will call on Him as long as I live."

Mary's friend begins to change, she becomes kinder toward others, respects her parents, and begins to love her future husband.

"Will you be my bridesmaid, Mary?"

"If I can, you know that I will."

"Oh, Mary, I need you so much!"

◆ ◆ ◆

Joachim's health begins to decline; often he hasn't strength to get up and go to work. Mary and Ana care for him tenderly, keeping him company, reading and praying with him until he falls asleep.

At the beginning of summer, when the chirping swallows begin their clamor in the sky, Joachim speaks what he has been mulling over for some time: they will go to Nazareth, to their old house, with its view of the valley, the orchard, fields and farm, relatives, and old friends. Full of joy, Mary laughs excitedly and immediately goes to tell Uncle Ben. Ana, more practical, begins to plan how to dismantle the house and organize the trip. That day, Joachim quits his job. He comes home serious.

"Little do men thank one for a lifetime of labor, Ana. God is the paymaster!"

Some things are sold, some given away; they deliberate about which belongings should be taken. One afternoon, Joachim appears with a young donkey that can hardly bear the packsaddle. It is gray, long-legged, with bright eyes, and on its forehead a white mark in the shape of a star. Mary receives him happily, runs her hand along the mane, and pats him fondly on the neck: "You are Donkey, a good donkey and hardworking. Uncle Ben, will you take care of him?"

The day of departure approaches, everything is ready and packed, the house is half-empty; it is the last night that they sleep there, all together on straw mats on the floor. Ana cannot sleep, there are so many memories that remain behind! Before dawn she rises; Mary wakes up and goes to her. They go out on the terrace together; the night is clear and serene.

"Look, Mother, a comet in the sky! What a beautiful sight!" Ana looks up, then pauses, contemplating it.

"Mother, they say that before the Messiah comes there will be signs in the heavens; could that be one?"

"Who knows? Daughter, let us glorify God who has made this universe so beautiful, and let us pray for the journey."

Joachim joins them to pray the Shemoneh Esrei, the eighteen short prayers of praise drawn from the Psalms and the Prophets expressing admiration and confidence toward the God of Israel.

The mule drivers arrive with mounts that stomp impatiently. Under the watchful eye of Uncle Ben, the loading of ready-prepared bundles begins. Ana passes out food and hot tea for everyone; the caravan is formed according to the order of preference of the mule drivers. Donkey, with an ill-fitting pack-saddle, is close to the head of the line. His ears stand up whenever Mary comes near, and he seems to look at her with moist eyes. Neighbors and relatives cluster around, greeting, chatting, hindering more than helping, yet distracting from this moment that does not lack nostalgia.

Joachim returns the keys to the landlord, takes one last walk around what has been his home, and mounts his mule. Mary gathers her hair, covers her head with a mantle, and quickly mounts the donkey that switches its tail complacently. Reins in hand, she observes her mother who hides tears behind her veil as she takes one final look at the house. After they invoke God's protection, they depart, much as Tobias did when he said goodbye to his son who was leaving with the Angel.

It is a long, exhausting trip because of the encumbrances. It is sometimes sunny, other times cloudy, with heat during the day and the cold at night. The dust raised by horsemen or the heavy carriages clings to their clothes and covers them to their eyelashes, but even so, Mary looks beautiful on the little donkey. The days' marches go by enlivened by the anticipation of arrival that reduces the journey's inconvenience.

Donkey behaves himself: to walk with such a mount spurs him on. Mary alternates places in the caravan to accompany one and then another. Always happy, her good humor lessens the fatigue and discomfort of the journey—her presence makes the going cheerful. As for Donkey, only a few soft touches from her heel make him hasten his pace or change direction, happy to obey her. On steep inclines he feels tired and unable to go on, but he looks up at the summit, makes another effort, until he arrives; his burden seems lighter on the downhill slope, and he is rewarded with a pat.

"Well, Donkey, we are the first to arrive. See how beautiful the valley looks from the top!"

One evening they can make out the first houses of Nazareth, illumined in the setting sun.

"Nazareth! Donkey, we are already close. Now you will rest."

As they enter the town, some dogs begin to bark; people come out to see the travelers with their numerous mounts. At the final hill, Joachim bids his first greeting. Donkey feels he just can't go any farther, lowers his head, tenses his muscles; his gait becomes shorter because of the slippery street.

"Just a little farther, Donkey, and we are there, then you will eat and rest. Come on, Donkey, up we go!"

They arrive at the old homestead where Uncle Ben, having gone ahead, awaits them: The floor is swept, the doors are open, the hearth and the lamps in the corridors are lit. On the table is a bowl of freshly picked figs, nectar still dripping; there is hot bread, cheese, and a pitcher of wine.

The travelers dismount, tired but happy. There is a whispering of angels who take up their watch upon this modest dwelling, in this little town in a land still in darkness.

The heat of the next day has not yet arrived, but everybody is already up. Mary walks happily throughout the house, kissing her parents, saying hello, laughing with everyone, her eyes sparkling. Swallows trill from their nest, joining her joy.

There is a knock at the door. It is Mary, her childhood friend, the one with black hair, gleaming eyes, and exuberant laugh. What happiness! At last they will be together—and they have so much to tell each other! After chatting a while, she, who is open and spontaneous, addresses her friend by her familiar name:

"Guess what, Miriam? I have a betrothed! His name is Alphaeus, but everyone calls him Cleophas. You will like him when you meet him. His parents are relatives of yours; they live in the first houses up the hill. Right now he is in the Basan Mountain bringing out wood. I really pray for him! He went with his brother, Joseph."

And they talk and laugh and their souls rejoice while they spend the morning hours unpacking the baggage.

"Will you come with me to the well tomorrow? I will come by early for you."

"I will go with you, Mary."

Ana, together with the faithful servant, who did not want to leave them, teaches Mary how to carry a water jar.

"It is more comfortable to carry it on the head, but more difficult to keep your balance. On the waist it's uncomfortable."

"I will carry it on my head."

Mary places a small round wrap of cotton on top of her head and practices walking around the patio; the servant applauds and Ana is thoughtful: *Mary is no longer a little child meant only for me.*

The clouds clear from the valley and the rising sun shines between the mountains. Her friend, Mary, arrives very early, with a happy voice and skill at managing the water jar. She praises the beauty of Miriam and the cleanliness of the house, and helps her place the jar on her head and gives her tips while making cheerful jokes. They leave after greeting Ana, who watches them and smiles. They arrive at the lower well of Nazareth, an ancient wellspring that has seen so many people come and go. A silent witness to many trysts and to countless dreams, to laughter and to sorrow, always scant but never dry.

Summer ends; autumn arrives. Early rains make clay and rivulets in the roads. Late one afternoon on a rainy day, Mary announces joyfully that her fiancé has arrived from the mountains; tomorrow he will be at the well to greet her.

Next day her friend arrives early, her eyes bright and joyful words on her lips. At the well they join other young women biding time for their turn. Soon Cleophas, together with his brother, Joseph, arrives. They greet the two women, and Miriam turns rosy. While Cleophas and his betrothed joke and laugh, she talks with Joseph, observes him; she is confused and moved by his voice, his demeanor, his manner. Never has she met anyone like him; she is especially impressed by his clear, forthright gaze, his strong and manly bearing, and his straightforward attitude. He seems reserved yet at the same time serene. She even has to be reminded that her jar is full!

Uncle Ben arrives; they say good-bye, smiling. As they climb the hill, Mary talks about Cleophas, "How good humored and strong he is!"

"Hey, Miriam, did you like Joseph?"

Mary colors, the crimson on her olive skin makes her more beautiful. Her dress is gathered around her, and the jar on her head wobbles.

"The things you say, Mary! I hardly know him!"

Mary tells Ana of her outing to the well and their encounter with the brothers. That night Ana notices that Mary is thoughtful, singing in a soft voice while she paces about. Her hesitations and blushes fade at nightfall.

The outings to the well continue, morning and afternoon. Some days Mary exchanges the flowers in her hair for colored ribbons. Her shawl is always clean, her dress ironed. One night, Mary tells her mother that she doesn't ever want to go back to the well.

"Why, daughter?"

"Mother, it has been my wish for many years to love only God, without there being a man between Him and me. I have met Joseph and I feel troubled."

"In love, daughter?"

"Oh, Mother, I don't know what to say to you."

Ana takes her hands in hers and looks at her flushed face.

"Daughter, you are completely free to do as you will. As your mother, I will give you the opinion that I have meditated in the presence of God and talked over with your father: We are old, you were born in our old age, a divine gift from God; soon we will leave this world. With whom will you abide, daughter? You need someone who will care for you and look out for you, someone who will protect your life in these very turbulent times. That is why we are going to speak to Joseph's parents, for we are very much in agreement that you should be his wife."

"Are you going to betroth me so soon?"

"My daughter, we believe we are doing what is best for you. These are the customs of Israel . . ."

Joachim, nearby, has heard these last words of Ana. Mary goes to him, hugs him, and gives him a kiss.

"Yes, child, I am very much in agreement with your mother. Joseph is good and is of our lineage; an honest, hard worker. If his parents accept, and Joseph wishes it, they will come to ask for your hand, and you will decide."

That afternoon, Mary looks serenely at the sunset through her small window; she dialogues with God: "My Lord, I will do what You want, whatever You say through my parents. By whichever means, I wish to love You with my whole heart and fulfill Your will."

The sky turns red from the rays of the sun reflected in the clouds that seem to form a crown of gold over the mountains. Night falls.

2

$\mathcal{S}$erene Hope

JOSEPH'S FAMILY IS NUMEROUS and congenial, united when they should be yet unhampered in seeking their own way; they are both laborers and artisans, having scarce land and huge needs. They are openhearted people—like their home, with restraint, they came down in the world due to the vicissitudes of history. The dwelling is ample, in disrepair because of the weathering of time and the neglect of men, located in nether Nazareth, facing the hill, its back to the valley.

Cleophas, some years older than Joseph, is average in height, thick of beard, with roguish eyes. He admires his brother and loves him dearly, even with the jokes he liked to play on him. Inconstant and adventurous, he dreamt of far off fortunes and had several times already left his home to go seek his fortune pursuing schemes that turned out more arduous than productive. Once back home, he told of his varied experiences with abundant exaggeration; then he would knuckle down to the field work until time had passed and fatigues been forgotten, setting him free to dream of new journeys.

Joseph is taller, with light eyes and a deep gaze, a gentle character although he can tell a good timely joke. An enthusiast of carpentry ever since he was a youngster, he has fine hands, aristocratic, yet calloused from work; a weatherworn face, a light beard. His deep and harmonious voice distinguishes him from his brothers. He works in a carpentry workshop where he tries his hand at everything: a plumb line mason, a blacksmith wielding a raw sledgehammer. With continuous working of the bellows, he forges the red iron until it reaches its form. When it's malleable he is able to shoe a horse with a good fit and in good time. When winter arrives he is ready to repair tile roofs or gutters, and when any gate, fence, or adobe wall needs repair, he skillfully mends it. He is known and loved by all.

In good weather he dedicates himself to working in the fields with his brothers; ever since he was young he has known about planting and sowing, harvests, rains, and drought. He has a little dog, "Doggie" he calls it, of rough hair and restless eyes, ready to beg and swift to hunt mice and agile to jump up the tree where the cat has sought refuge. Faithful to Joseph, he sleeps at his door at night and in the afternoons waits for him, head resting on the floor, eyes unmoving.

One winter, close to the warm flickering of the big kitchen hearth, next to the bustle of young and old, Cleophas confides to Joseph a new project: to go and cut wood from the timberland of Bashan, on the border with Perea: a mountainous region of encircled forests as yet unexploited, big cedars of fine woods and red hearts, rivers that drop through ravines, beasts that terrorize with nighttime roars, dangerous men that prowl in the valleys. They are organizing a party of cutters to go in spring and return in autumn; the pay is good compared to what they are used to earning.

"There are risks. That doesn't scare you, does it?"

Joseph thinks about it and builds up hopes. He is already twenty-four years old, wants to learn, get to know other lands, become more knowledgeable about the wood that is the pillar of his work, how to work it, its qualities. His parents look upon them with anxiety but respect their decisions. Two sons that leave home at the same time! On the other hand, they will know how to take care of one another. Joseph is a serious, conscientious, hard worker. Cleophas is impetuous, chatterbox and inconstant, as quick to anger as to smile. They complement each other.

Winter flies by like the gray clouds that carry the spring waters. The brothers start preparing the things for whose hauling they will use the old mule—with more callouses than hair—lent them by their father. The gear includes well-sharpened axes with handles made to measure of cured olivewood, machetes, canvases waterproofed with tar against the rains, a tent.

A windy blue sky bending the tops of the trees announces the day of departure. Joseph and Cleophas have a good breakfast and say good-bye to their parents and siblings. They skillfully saddle the mule and, accompanied by Doggie, head to the town square, where they meet with other companions in adventures who are bearing their axes and overflowing leather pouches. Before leaving town, Cleophas says good-bye to Mary, his fiancée, who remains tearful between smiles and good-byes; then they set out toward the east, happy and full of hopes.

The next day they reach the River Jordan, full and dirty from the spring rains, and set up camp next to a ford. Some fishermen who are throwing nets sell them fresh fish that they roast over a fire. As evening falls, they eat in peace under the failing light of the setting sun. The first crickets sing; frogs croak nearby in coarse, off-key tones. Nearby some donkeys graze. Cleophas sees them and starts laughing:

"Do you remember, Joseph—when we were still kids—when we caught donkeys to make ourselves into invincible riders in the eyes of the girls playing close by?

Joseph does remember and smiles. The girls were playing next to the river, not paying much attention to them; so they went to the young donkeys, untied them and lightly mounted them, then set them to racing with shouts and heel kicks. Cleophas's mount threw its rider upon reaching a mud puddle, and he lay there full length. Joseph's finished its crazy gallop some yards further on and was on the point of throwing him too, when he dismounted and ran to help his humiliated brother, now exiting the puddle while the amused girls watched, among whom this following exclamation was heard:

"Look, Miriam," exclaimed one, "look at that face!"

Joseph, distracted, was now contemplating Miriam's face, exceedingly beautiful, rose-tinted, with eyes full of laughter: Miriam, Miriam. Often as a boy he recalled that face and that name and was filled with youthful dreams of love and tenderness. What had become of that girl?

Supper over, Joseph says his prayers while looking at the tranquil river, so linked to the history of his people, like himself in turmoil but moving on toward something that lay ahead.

"What, Lord, are you preparing for us? What do you want from me? I am willing to give it to you, my God." He falls asleep under the branches of a tree with the stars above him.

The next day, as low fog rises from the river and the sun's first rays appear in the east, they cross the ford, robes rolled up to their waists, loads on their heads, feet groping the slippery pebbles below. The mule stumbles, snorts, but he is firmly held by Joseph. Doggie paddles at the side with head held high. Reaching the opposite bank, they put their shoes on, adjust the saddle strap and their own mounts and set off toward Pella. The road rises, falls, twists, but gradually goes upward.

At nightfall they arrive at Jerash, spread out among hills and forests. They stay on the outskirts, under a big holm oak that gives shade to merchants at fairs. The contractor awaits them, an older man, strong, weather-beaten, with two sons. With them are muleteers and a drove of mules, along with bundles from which giant saws stick out. Curious children and women approach with their baskets, offering to sell them food. Joseph and his companions greet them, make themselves comfortable, and rest. They drink strong tea heated on the nearby fire, and when the sun sets they negotiate prices, living conditions, the give-and-take of contractors and contracted. Cleophas drives a hard bargain, hints at heading back home. Joseph looks on silently. Finally they come to an agreement and embrace. A kiss closes the deal. They sup happily and retire.

They wake at dawn, stiff, after a bad night of howling dogs, the kicking of mules. The contractor and his sons arrive, having spent the night in the house of friends who gave them something hot and filling to eat. They cross the picturesque mountain town, with many wood houses and corrals, smoke smelling of pine, roads of hardened clay, people with rosy cheeks and curious looks. Before leaving the town they buy provisions and take them to the mules. Children and curious elders look on. Some dogs get into fights with other neighborhood dogs. Doggie barks a lot, but his aggressiveness is more bluff than action.

They head uphill as the sun grows stronger. The view widens, the village below them, the wide valley behind them, and before them the green mountains over which clouds pass. The road narrows, becomes a footpath, full of hoof prints left by the beasts year after year carrying wood from the immense forests. Streams cross the dry clay of the path, dense ravines covered with weeds line the sides. Up and around and around they go until they reach the crest, their strength nearly exhausted. They stop to spend the night in some rickety shacks. Smoke from the fires irritates their eyes, making them water.

In the half-light of early morning they resume their journey. Joseph admires the slopes from the advantage of higher perspective; now the valley lies far down and is covered by the clouds from which solitary peaks emerge. The first large trees good for wood appear. Pure air whispers in the branches, fills their lungs, and lifts their hearts to God. Cleophas never stops talking or laughing, rebuking the mules when they stall and daydreaming aloud. The effort of the trek with heavy loads unifies the group. They become friends before living together.

In late afternoon they reach the plateau. Here they set up camp, close to the stream that flows in the underbrush. Tall hills surround them. Big cedars raise their tops to the heavens reddened by the setting sun. The fire crackles. Profound silence becomes prayer. Well wrapped in his poncho, Joseph comes out of his tent, prays, talks to the Lord, contemplating those dark hills where he will work tomorrow and that starry sky where the glory of God shines. Doggie jumps at his side, runs, comes back, at his feet still, his head between his paws. He isn't cold, is he?

No, he has Joseph.

They wake up with the sunlight already in their tents. Soon they will be ready to climb the mountain with its humid underbrush and soil soft with the fallen leaves of centuries. They follow the path, reaching the summit. Here the wind blows even more strongly and the opposite valley comes into view: lands of cedar, mountain after mountain, covered in trees, blue mounds in the background stretching to the horizon. Puffing, the contractor arrives. He doesn't stop to look at the landscape but goes to the splendid cedar that rises nearby with wind-driven clouds passing over it. They clear the base with their machetes, and the giant trunk appears with all the strength of its species and the grandeur of its age. The axes begin to cleave this noble wood that jumps in splinters without complaint. Joseph is skillful, yet even so his arms tire, his back aches. Between strokes, he takes a breath, dries the perspiration from his forehead, then returns to the task, rhythmically alternating blows that echo along the gorge. The wood begins to creak, silencing the birds that fly away. The tree slowly slants like a wounded giant, falls amid crashing branches, and thunders to the ground. In the silence the pounding of other axes is heard. They scramble over the trunk, prune it, begin cutting ten-by-ten pieces.

The morning passes, fatigue sets in, the axe seems made of lead, the handle wounds hands to the point of blistering them. In the afternoon, that beautiful specimen whose crown had soared above, is dragged in pieces down to the slope. Pushed and pulled by mules, the logs reach the plateau and rest there like the bones of a gigantic animal.

Night falls. Men drop exhausted around the hearth. Joseph still has enough energy to sharpen axes, his and Cleophas's, while Cleophas soaks his hands in saltwater and at the same time half-jokingly rues of having come to this mountain.

The new day dawns, wet, gray, airless. No chirping of birds. It's time to saw the trunks. Cleophas doesn't even move when Joseph tries to wake him up; instead he wraps himself even more tightly in his blanket. At last the sun begins to shine. He manages to rise.

Shifts for cutting are assigned. Joseph marks his trunk. The big beams, marked, will be brought down with the mules.

Meanwhile his companion has been digging a deep ditch under the trunk, steadied by scaffolding. They bring the big saw. Joseph above, his companion beneath, they start a rhythmic to and fro, muscles obeying will. Tough, monotonous work that identifies man with his Creator and the world bequeathed for him to transform. Joseph elevates his thoughts and opens a contemplative dialogue as the trunk begins to open, exposing its red core. He goes into the trench, puts on an old, wide-brimmed hat, and begins pulling the great saw. Sawdust falls on him, covering his clothes, identifying him with the soil he treads. Hours and hours pass of work well done, in company with God as well as man.

The days follow one after another routinely. Saw alternates with axe as Joseph unites his will even further to the will of God.

The evenings are happy, the body's weariness lessens, and camaraderie springs up amid the jokes of these rustic men, joined in isolation in a common task. Cleophas creates laughter and sometimes annoyance, being quick to blow and blow to renew the fire but not moving a finger to maintain it.

Joseph is tidy, leaving each thing in its proper place, clean, ready to be used again, looking after things big and small. From him comes strength that gives confidence to his companions and makes them respect him; he is always willing to lend a helping hand and show how a task might be done in a better way without offending the careless one. He helps with the forge to sharpen the axes or the teeth of the saws. He is especially appreciated for treating wounds with herbs and plasters, so skillful that he amazes them. Hardest to cure is Cleophas, since no one can tell if he is ill for sure or just lazy.

From his youth, Joseph has acquired good habits at home. Before supper he bathes in the stream, whether it is cold or hot. Just seeing it, says Cleophas, gives him goose bumps.

❖ ❖ ❖

Days pass like spring clouds laden with water. Work tempers muscles and strengthens wills. One night it rains steadily, and at daybreak everything is wet; fog drifts at ground level, the tools are wet, the trunks slippery. Joseph and his companion take the saw to the cut begun the day before. The farmhand—a young worker from Nazareth, quiet and helpful—from beneath gives a strong pull to begin, the trunk—badly settled on the ground now loose because of the rain—gives way and falls on him, striking him heavily on the head and knocking him down. Joseph leaps into the trench and with difficulty hauls him out and brings him near the tent.

The boy gazes vacantly into space, bleeding from the corners of his mouth. Others gather around them. Joseph arranges his clothes, covers him well, and prays for the boy, who assents with his eyes. He asks God to spare his life, but this slowly leaves the youth, like the shreds of fog rising before them under the force of the sun. He looks around him, trembles, sighs, and dies with his hands between Joseph's. Everyone falls silent, even the farthest axes, as the wind and the bird that sings the way he used to imitate.

A large, manly tear rolls down Joseph's cheek. Cleophas also cries and deplores the youth's bad luck. They close his eyes and remain close, hardly speaking. They no longer work; they mourn. Joseph looks at his pale face and reflects: *Lord, this could have been me; how brief is life. Death stalks us, our existence ends in a moment. We have little time to deserve you, love you, do good, we are like the flowers in this field, here and the next day gone. Alas, for his parents! They won't see him again. He left home full of hope, he won't return. It is a great mystery, life, yet a greater mystery is death; Our God, we are yours and to You we go sooner or later. . . .*

Downcast, they eat and take turns digging the grave on the other side of the stream. At sundown, in the fading light, his companions bury him with tears in their eyes. Afterward, they hardly speak.

◆ ◆ ◆

Rainy days come, with moments of sunlight interspersed. The work continues. The mules have no rest in the endless dragging downhill of long beams and the return uphill with foodstuffs. One afternoon, the cutters on the extreme north of the mountain come, excitedly announcing that they have sighted a herd of wild rams coming down to drink at the cascade. Questions, memories, expectations, and plans to hunt greet the news. The contractor gives permission, hoping to dispel the mournful feelings after the death of their companion. They prepare rustic spears with tips hardened at the fire, then go out at midnight, by moonlight, to surprise the animals, placing themselves here and there in the ravine to await them. But the rams sense their presence and do not appear. After a fruitless wait, numbed and uncomfortable, they return at daybreak. A few days later, the wind changes and they decide to try again. Cleophas is the most enthusiastic, having already forgotten the failure of the previous vigil. Once again they arrive at the ravine after midnight, silently distribute themselves, wait. "Look up at the sky, Joseph: A comet!"

Joseph looks up and sees the comet in all its grandeur, tracing a blazing trail across the firmament.

"What a beautiful spectacle, Cleophas; let's give thanks to God that we are seeing it."

"Joseph, they say that before the coming of the Messiah, great signs will be seen in the heavens. Do you think this is one? I hope He comes soon."

"God willing, Cleophas."

At early dawn, to the thrill of the hunters, the herd appears. The men are so quiet they can only hear their hearts beating. At a signal, they throw themselves on the rams, running and shouting. Most of the beasts get away, but two small ones lie fallen, while another one gores and kicks amid bleaks until they manage to bring it down.

That night, while they are eating the roasted meat by the light of the fire, they hear the deafening roars of a mountain lion. The mules are frightened, and they must go to the corrals to calm them.

Summer comes and with it good weather. The scrub dries, the afternoons lengthen. The birds that had nested in the great trees felled by their axes trill incessantly, while birds ousted from their nests still flit about grieving. The work goes on. Many of the cedars are converted into beams or boards. Joseph comes to know these woods better and better, their veins, their hardness, their knots. He continues to help his companions, having gained their trust. They listen to him attentively when he speaks to them of God, of good and evil, of the work that binds us to God's creation. Cleophas decides always to pray before the day ends. He is amazed at his brother, loves him more every day, and admires him especially when he takes care of the sick. What patience he has with them! He does it naturally, as though not doing anything special, with good humor.

One day in the afternoon the dogs bark furiously, screams are heard, a shadowy figure is visible in the branches. They come close, axes ready, and spy a man, half-naked and bearded, trembling and numb who can barely hold himself up. They bring him down and study him. The man tells them he is lost, has not eaten for days, and has approached to beg for something. His wrists and ankle bear the marks of irons; his back is furrowed with the scars of ancient whiplashes. A fugitive slave. The sons of the contractor tell him to go away, threatening him with the dogs. They want no problems, and he may be hunted. Joseph intervenes, tells them he takes responsibility for letting the man stay. They grudgingly allow it and go back to their tents. Cleophas has kept silent. "Brother, you are an idealist," he says. Joseph gives the slave, now warming himself next to the fire, something to eat and lends him dry clothes while he devours the food. How much suffering there is in this poor life! It's a consequence of human cruelty and arbitrariness. Aren't we all God's children and born free?

Now the man tells something of his story. He is from a country in Asia Minor, made prisoner in a battle with the Romans and sold as a slave to a Jewish merchant who brought him to Jerusalem. There he learned the language. But the merchant's sons mistreated him unspeakably, until one afternoon he fled. Living like a beast, walking only at night, sleeping hidden during the day, he came to these mountains exhausted and lost. He had a wife, a little girl, parents . . . what had become of them? He's been away nearly ten years. Joseph listens closely. "Rest here peacefully," he says. "Take this ram's skin."

The good weather continues. At midday it is hot and bees buzz. Crickets sing at night. One Saturday the slave—to whom Joseph has just given a haircut—tells him he has seen fish downstream and will teach them to catch them. Together with Cleophas and the others, they go toward the river. Approaching a pool they see the fish rushing to hide under the rocks. The slave gets into the water and, feeling his way, slowly lowers his hands. Water up to his chin, he feels in the hollows of the stones. Shortly, he holds up a fish and tosses it to the bank. Joseph gets in and searches among the hollows eager to feel a fish between his hands. The others do the same, and they go pool by pool, capturing fish amid shouts of glee and exclamations because of the cold water. In the end, they bathe under a cascade while a dozen fish linked by a vine threaded through their gills hang from a branch shining in the sun.

They rest during the afternoon. The slave, now increasingly fond of Joseph, talks to him about his life. Joseph listens to him with pleasure—it is a gift forged since youth and practiced with everybody. In his homeland, the man had a small farm, friends, and affection; at sundown he liked to sing for his little daughter. He lost everything in a few days, and now he doesn't believe in any god. Joseph talks to him of his God, the Father of mercy and love and forgiveness, Creator of those red-tinted heavens, the darkening mountain, the flowers that surround them: an indivisible, pure, invisible Spirit, in whom we abide, move, and exist. He speaks of our immortal soul that nobody can destroy, of the choice of the Jewish people, of the prayers composed over the centuries in His praise. Cleophas also listens, but unenthusiastically.

"Joseph, you worry about everything."

Summer fades, the days become shorter, the nights freshen. A few times they are unable to work because of the strong storms with thunder reverberating against the mountains, hail that bounces off the tarpaulins, lightning flashing around them. Hunched up inside their tents, they implore God's protection. The stream echoes the sound of the rocks dragged by the current. Doggie whines, frightened, under Joseph's cape. The slave takes the opportunity to finish carving an orangewood staff with many exquisite filigrees. Then he gives it to Joseph.

"Joseph, I hope it flowers in your hands like the one you told me flowered in Aaron's."

One morning the tents are white, covered with frost. Winter is coming. The contractor decides to finish. That day they no longer cut trees. They only saw the last of the boards to be taken by the mules. Then they begin dismantling the camp. They pick wild fruits and nuts that they roast at nighttime over the blaze, and they are happy. One morning, the mules having returned, they collect the tools and cast one last glance at the surrounding hills, wounded in many places where trees formerly stood.

Joseph takes the slave aside. They walk in silence to a promontory.

"Over there lies your land. Several times I have shown you how to get to it, and under which stars you will find it at this time of the year. You are free to return—with the help of God—or to come with us."

The slave looks at him, eyes brimming with tears.

"I don't want to leave you, Joseph; you have treated me well, with kindness; you have restored my faith in myself, in men, in God. May He reward you forever. But I wish to return to my own land. I may not get there, but maybe I will."

He embraces Joseph, sobbing shamelessly.

"God will not abandon you. Pray to him every day. Hate no one. And never stop singing. Good-bye."

They return to the group, and the men say good-bye to the slave, giving him useful presents for his journey. These are rough folk but good-hearted. They take their leave. At the first bend in the road, they take one last glance back at the plateau and at the slave, who is waving good-bye.

❖ ❖ ❖

The return journey is quick and pleasurable. Molded by the rough work of the past month, their bodies do not tire; the men do not even notice their heavy loads. One night they spy prowlers behind some hills and decide to put their savings in the mule's packsaddles, well hidden in the rough manes.

Coming to a ford over the Jordan, they pitch a small tent, light the fire, and after eating in harmony, rest. At midnight Doggie barks furiously. They awake and, seeing several armed men approaching, take to their heels. Joseph leaps to the mule, cuts the bridle, and gives it a strong slap. Behind him he hears screams and feels a sharp pain in the waist. Running upriver, he is closely followed by Cleophas, who does not stop cursing the bandits under his breath. They fall among bushes, rise, fall again, scrape their hands and faces. Finally they have to stop due to the thickness of the vegetation. They rest.

Doggie howls pitifully. Joseph notices that he has a long, shallow cut from which blood flows copiously. Cleophas dresses it with a bandage as best as he can. What has become of their companions? They whistle, imitating the song of the cuckoo in the mountains. From not too far away comes an answer. One of their companions approaches. He has an enormous head wound bleeding over his face and chest. Joseph bandages him with his shirt and rallies him when he is about to faint. Night thickens, a bad night. Chilled to the bone, they slap themselves and keep jumping so as not to lose heat.

"And what if they have taken our mule and savings?"

"Don't worry Cleophas, we are alive; let's thank God."

Daybreak comes at last, and light fills them with hope. Carefully they creep toward the forest's edge. From afar, they see the assailants, attempting to seize the mule, which repeatedly trots away skittishly; the old mule with its packsaddle won't let itself be caught.

"Damn sons of . . . !"

"Be quiet, Cleophas, there is naught to be gained by cursing; better to pray!"

Finally the assailants pick up their gear and leave. Cautiously, the fugitives emerge from their hiding place and come close to the ford of the river. The other youths appear, terrified but unharmed. The bandits have left nothing. Searching the shrubs, Joseph finds his staff. They look for the mule, which, though still skittish, lets itself be caught by them.

A big caravan arrives at the river. They join it warming themselves by the fires and buying clothing and food. Lifting up the wounded man onto the mule, they cross the Jordan.

"Cleophas, there is one advantage to having been left with nothing: We are not carrying any load."

Sensing the return, Doggie barks happily. Cleophas talks about his wedding plans. He wants to settle down, no more adventures, and someone with gentle hands to cook him his meals, no more horrid camp stews! Joseph laughs and everybody joins in. The sun breaks through the clouds.

Next day Nazareth lies before them. Doggie goes before them joyfully; the old mule quickens its pace. Reaching the house, they say good-bye to their mates, shared work having made them friends. Joseph promises that he will tell the parents of the dead boy. A sad task, to be faced as soon as possible. Brothers and nephews greet them with shouts of joy. Their parents hug them effusively.

"Welcome, children. Praised be God. How much we have waited and prayed for you!"

They go into their house, tired, more mature, happy once again to be among their own.

◆ ◆ ◆

After a couple of days Cleophas proposes to go in search of his betrothed, Mary. He invites Joseph to accompany him. Joseph is reluctant but agrees to please his brother. He puts on his good clothes. The morning is fresh, sunny, and they walk leisurely, saying hello to friends and acquaintances, shoulders thrown back, tanned by the sun, hair and beards recently trimmed.

Mary is at the well with other girls, filling jars amid laughter and timid looks. Cleophas greets his intended, who blushes and responds full of happiness; Mary reintroduces her friend Miriam. Cleophas talks and talks, tells about his journey. Joseph cannot take his eyes from Mary's friend. He feels his heart is bursting; his whole being is moved. He is awkward when he helps her place the water jar on her head. Her hair, under the veil, smells of flowers.

"Good-bye, until this afternoon . . ."

Cleophas claps his brother on the shoulder.

"What do you think of my girl? Don't you think she is pretty? Those dimples in her cheeks when she laughs. . . . What's wrong with you? Can it be you have fallen for Miriam? Yes, she is very beautiful. Good friends Mary chooses! But what's wrong with you, Joseph? You are as red as this carnation."

In the afternoon Joseph asks his parents about Miriam.

"We know her well; she is the daughter of Joachim and Ana, distant relatives of ours. They arrived from Jerusalem not long ago. Joachim used to work in the temple as administrator of the gate of the sheep. They own some houses further up and some lands in the valley. Mary was born to them when they were elderly; they all say she is an admirable young woman, beautiful, unassuming, and good."

"Mother, how old can she be?"

"Close to eighteen. She was born when I was expecting your sister. Many summers they came down from Jerusalem to spend some months here, always looked after by Ben, a relative of Ana who doesn't let her out of his sight, come rain or shine. Joachim is a very hard worker, honest and pious, now somewhat sickly. That's why he retired from his work. Ana is a great woman."

Cleophas intervenes to tell his parents he wishes to marry Mary forthwith.

"I want to settle down. I'm going into business. I'm going to be a great trader. What do you think of going to ask her parents tomorrow?"

At mid-afternoon the brothers, well-groomed, go to the well. Some young girls start to arrive. Cleophas jokes with them. At last Miriam and Mary arrive. Seeing her again, Joseph feels a lump in his throat. She lowers her eyes and greets him. Cleophas talks to Mary, who laughs unabashedly. He proposes matrimony. He is eager to settle down, start a home. Besides, he loves her intensely. How much he has thought of her during those nights in the mountains!

Miriam, who sees that Joseph doesn't dare talk, asks about his woodcutting work. Joseph answers, feeling Miriam's eyes and her full attention on him.

"Hey, Miriam your jar was filled long ago!" say her companions. She retrieves it, helped by Joseph, and they both laugh.

"Miriam, do you like it here in Nazareth?"

Now it is she who talks in a sweet voice that to Joseph seems the most harmonious sound in this world. He forgets his surroundings and does not notice that the sun is going down behind his shoulder nor hear the voices of Cleophas or Mary.

Oh Lord, what a lovely creature has come from Your hands! How is it I had not discovered her before!

Joseph feels his young, noble, good heart has fallen in love with Miriam to the ultimate fibers of his being. The intensity of the moment is finally broken by Mary saying they have to go; it has grown late.

"Until tomorrow, Miriam, God be with you." He helps her put the water on her head.

"God bless you, Joseph."

The brothers slowly go up the hill.

"You heard, Joseph, she said yes to me. God willing we'll have a wedding next month. . . . Hey! Are you listening to me?"

That night Joseph decides to open his own carpentry shop. He will spend all his savings buying tools and wood, and he will work independently.

Days go by, journeys to the well continue, dreams become concrete projects. Joseph speaks of his workshop, Cleophas of his commerce.

Mary is very enthusiastic; laughs and laughs. Miriam listens and meditates.

❖ ❖ ❖

One of Joseph's relatives has some good, arable land. Having done some late sawing, tomorrow he will begin to harvest, with the brothers doing piecework. They invite their friends to come along and glean, as for centuries has been a tradition with Jewish women.

The next day at dawn the two brothers are ready—sickles sharpened, clothes rolled up—for the hard task of cutting wheat together with other field hands and the uncle observing the work. Often they look toward the road. Finally they see a group of young girls appear, accompanied by Ben, Ana's relative, with sacks ready. Joseph's heart misses a beat. There is Miriam. She puts her mantle to one side, gathers her hair in a small straw hat, and begins to pick up sprigs fallen from the reapers' hands. Next to her Mary winks and smiles at Cleophas (he's at risk of cutting off his own hand for looking at her). Joseph also looks between breaths.

The morning passes quickly despite the hard work. The laborers bend toward the earth rutted by furrows, arms tensed by the cutting. At midday they gather under a big oak. The uncle brings them water, wine, and provisions.

"Good work, boys, though it seems many sprigs have escaped your hands," he says looking at the bulging sacks of the young girls, now preparing the food upon a tablecloth.

They lunch happily and talk. Miriam, face flushed by the sun, unties her long hair for a while. Cleophas announces his forthcoming marriage to Mary, who blushes before the congratulations of her companions. Joseph tells Miriam he wishes to pay his respects to her parents and, if he may, continue to call on her. Now Miriam is the one who blushes.

"Joseph, I will tell my parents and do what they tell me."

The work goes on in the afternoon. Before the sun begins to set, the girls pick up their things, wave good-bye, and go with Uncle Ben, who helps them carry their sacks. The field looks empty. The sun reaches the farther mountains, and the reapers stop working. They return, singing in the twilight.

"Joseph, I never heard you sing so loud. I didn't think you could . . ."

A frightened roadrunner rushes before them. Up there on the heights, Nazareth with its trembling lights resembles a fragment of the starry sky.

Cleophas's wedding is an event in the town. His family is numerous, and Mary's more so—good reason to come together and celebrate in the peace of God. The day is cold, without wind. Since daybreak, Joseph and Cleophas have been greeting friends and family. Their elderly parents are happy to see their firstborn married and quietly tell relatives it looks as if Joseph may soon do the same.

In the afternoon everybody goes uphill toward Mary's house. At the door are the virgins with lit lamps. There is Miriam, with her new dress and a flower garland on her head. Joseph looks at her as he passes, and she lowers her eyes. Everyone goes in. The girls dance to the music of rustic musicians, off-key and cheerful. They sing, asking God to bless the spouses. Joseph has eyes only for Miriam. He picks out her voice from the others, and his love for her blazes even stronger. He will speak to her parents and ask for her in marriage; he does not want for work, he has hands to support her, and a heart to love her all their lives.

A few days later, he goes with his parents to Miriam's house; he is nervous yet tranquil. Ben opens the door. The house is spick-and-span, with freshly cut flowers. Joachim and Ana are expecting them and greet them affectionately; they talk of trivial matters until, supported by her husband Jacob, Joseph's mother brings up their purpose in coming. Joseph seems glued to the chair, not daring to raise his eyes. Ana approaches him and, taking his hands and looking him in the eyes, says:

"Joseph, we didn't expect you to come so soon to ask for Mary's hand. As far as we are concerned there are no impediments, but it's for her to decide. Even though she is my daughter, she is altogether marvelous. She has never given us cause for concern. She is happy, a hard worker, right-living, good with everybody. Treat her well. She is a piece of our heart, the best part of our life."

"Lady Ana, before God I promise you I will honor and cherish her as long as I live, for in the short time I've known her I have learned to love her with all my heart."

Joachim now says: "Joseph, if Mary consents, we prefer that you become engaged next month and that the wedding be in one year. That way we will have her during that time, helping her prepare her dowry while you become established in your work." And everyone says yes. They are in agreement. Ana calls Mary, who enters with lowered eyes.

"Mary, Joseph's parents have asked us to approve your becoming his wife. We agree. You know well that we would have wished to have you with us more years. Do you consent?"

"Mother, I will do whatever you decide."

Joseph's parents hug her and kiss her. Joseph's mother addresses her softly: "Daughter, Joseph is the best of my children, a hard worker. He is a man of prayer. All who know him love him."

They exchange presents, and talk about what according to ancient custom the "mohar" should be. They eat dinner, their hearts lighten, and they say good-bye with the moon in the sky.

Joseph now may visit Mary at her home every day. His love deepens the more he knows her. Once, when they are alone for a few moments, Mary says to him:

"Joseph, before we become husband and wife I must tell you of my wish to remain a virgin, to dedicate my life to God, to prayer and doing good to others."

"Mary, I love you so much that I will respect your will. God will tell us what we should do."

The day of the betrothal arrives. Something strange in Nazareth happens. The ground is white from a light snow that fell during the night, as if this were nature's way of celebrating the day by placing an immaculate mantle upon land, houses, and trees. In the afternoon, Joseph comes with his parents—all bundled up—and brothers and relatives. They are joined by Cleophas and Mary, themselves supremely happy at Joseph's choice. They arrive at Joachim's house, warm and smelling of pine resin and incense. Mary appears extremely beautiful, in a new dress with flowers in her hair beneath a white veil. Her friend Mary applauds her joyfully. Joseph receives congratulation from friends and relatives.

Everyone falls silent during the simple ceremony before parents and witnesses. Mary and Joseph come forward and express their desire to join in holy matrimony. Joseph takes Mary's hand and holds it between his while they make their declaration.

As a token of his commitment, Joseph gives her an old gold ring his mother had kept. "This ring is evidence that you shall be my wife according to the Law of Moses and of Israel," he says.

Once the ceremony is over, everybody congratulates them. Then they go to eat, happy and chattering, with that simplicity of humble folk and hard workers who have little to offer and nothing to hide.

Doggie has been waiting impatiently, shivering by the door. When no one is looking, he slips in to join the celebration. Mary gives him a snack.

It begins to snow again. A pale moon appears amid softly falling snowflakes.

3

The Shade Tree

UNCLE BEN WAS A DISTANT RELATIVE of Ana, of indefinite age and medium height, with graying hair and strong hands. He had a sincere yet somewhat timid gaze and an awkward gait, the consequence of an old wound. He had tried his hand at many things in life, none of them permanent: soldier, sailor, merchant; now he was homeless and without family. Like a ship without rigging after a tempest, he came to dock at Joaquin's house soon after Mary's birth, and thanks to his obliging nature and humbleness, there he remained, more friend than server.

It was when Ana allowed him to look after little Mary that he began to feel a great love for her, which grew and overflowed when she began to speak and called him "Inkly Ben," gazing at him with her lovely, lively eyes so full of life. His life changed; it now held meaning, a reason for being: to take care of that girl growing every day more graceful and comely. At night he kept vigil next to her crib, ears cocked for any sound. If she coughed, he would not sleep. When she played, he, amid his tasks of cleaning the house or storing grain from the harvest, never lost sight of her for long. Ana scolded him fondly and said he spoiled Mary too much, that if it were up to him, her feet would never touch the ground. Uncle Ben kept his peace while thinking: *If it were a slice of the moon she asked me for, why, I would up and fetch it from heaven for her.*

41

Best of all were those summer days when they went to Nazareth. Early in the morning he would go to the fields, cut fresh flowers, encircle them with thyme, take them to her door, and then, with eyes aglow, watch as she smelled and praised them. He indulged her to the length of his tenderness, raising her up in his strong hands so that she might pick the best figs from the old fig tree next door or look at the baby doves in the turtledove's nest. He would bring her the first clusters of grapes from the vine, the first blackberries from the bramble, or some nestling carried safely from its home. And he would linger to watch while she ran around the patio of the old house with other little girls. Sometimes he went with them to the river to catch tadpoles and little fish. They dove into the water, laughed, and returned with feet and hair all wet. Uncle Ben always managed to find them some seasonal fruit that they ate on their way back in the late afternoons.

He was an uncomplicated soul, very much like those rough garden leaves that provide a contrast with beautiful flowers—or like those solitary relatives who find a niche in homes and serve humbly all their lives, lacking a light of their own and merely reflecting the light of others, was enough for them.

One day, when Mary was barely seven, they were coming back from the fields when a big snake darted out and threw itself on Mary. Uncle Ben swiftly drove it away with a stick, but Mary remained frightened and weepy.

"It wanted to bite my foot!" she repeated.

Uncle Ben had to carry her home in his arms the rest of the way, her face buried in his shoulder. In the evening, she wanted no supper. Uncle Ben slept several nights at the foot of her bed until the dread went away.

When it was time to thresh, Mary and Uncle Ben loved to get up on the thresher—that rustic wooden platform with big pegs at its base that the donkey drew round and around. In the end they climbed down, took up the sieves and amid spirited laughter launched the grains of wheat into the afternoon wind to separate them from the hay.

During winter afternoons, Uncle Ben made things with strips of leather, at which he was most expert, his hardened hands shaping the leather—soaked in herbal waters—into shoes, belts, pouches, even rustic saddles. Mary looked at him occasionally and asked him to make things for her. Learning passages of Sacred Scripture read to her by Ana, she would faultlessly recite them to him from memory.

"Uncle Ben, do you want me to tell you what the angel said when he bade Tobias farewell?"

This caused great admiration in Uncle Ben and everybody else in the house. Sometimes Joachim came close to hear her with the ancient rolls of Sacred Scripture in his hand to verify the phrases, and so did Ana, who still had a wonderful memory. Hearing her sing enchanted Uncle Ben as well as all the family and friends. Mary had a sweet and vibrant voice that at twelve years old became firm and gave a delightful lilt to the traditional songs of the people of Israel that young girls had sung for centuries. Her cousins and other girls also sang when they visited, and the singing resembled a prayer praising God. Uncle Ben would then hide behind the column so as not to be seen showing the emotion that he felt.

In the summer, when they came back from Jerusalem, they frequently went out to the fields with Joachim to help him in the farm work. Mary was ready early and looked forward to any task. Joachim had some fields on the skirts of the mountain over which he allowed the grass to grow in the winter rains. The first mowing was in June. The hay was piled up around a thick pole driven into the ground, and when the pile was ready, Uncle Ben helped Mary and the other children climb on top and slide down the grass amid shouts and laughter. At summer's end, they hoisted the drying hay onto the old oxcart. Mary happily climbed on top with the other children, and they would drive slowly to the squeaking of the wooden cart wheels and the urging of Uncle Ben who spurred on the oxen with his pike while he looked up with smiling eyes at the cart's cargo.

❖ ❖ ❖

Years went by. Mary became a woman and gathered her hair under a veil. The news that they would move to Nazareth because Joachim had finished his work at the temple enormously pleased Uncle Ben. There he could be of greater service to Mary. He knew the country, the seasons, the time for each flower and fruit. He didn't like the fact that shortly after their arrival Mary began going to the well with her cousins for drinking water; the hill was steep and he could easily fetch it. Ana told him no, Mary should do it like the other young women of the town for she was no longer a child. Uncle Ben sulked for three days. Some young men went there to see the young girls, and one in particular named Joseph couldn't tear his eyes from Mary and blushed before her like a boy, although he was already a man with a full beard.

Uncle Ben liked Joseph as he saw him more frequently, but he sensed in the depths of his being that Mary, the little one of his life, would be taken away from him. And so it was. Autumn had not yet begun, it was a little after the Feast of Tabernacles— that year very joyful and well attended because of the good harvests—that Mary herself gave him the news.

"Uncle Ben, today Joseph's parents are coming to ask for my hand in marriage. I shall do what my parents ask me, for they will know God's will."

Uncle Ben's heart sank, and he didn't know what to say.

"Mary, my little one you are so young . . . you like to pray, talk to God, and care for everybody—your parents and this house and these fields."

"Uncle Ben, I am going to do whatever my parents say, as is the custom." Then looking at him tenderly: "I won't go far; Joseph is of these parts."

From early dawn, Uncle Ben worked hard for the betrothal, cleaning the house from top to bottom, fetching water, picking up leaves from the patio, watering the plants. But he was not at the ceremony; he left the house when Joseph's parents arrived with his relatives and did not return until well into the night. On his way out, from the corner of his eye, he caught a glimpse of

Mary with Ana who was fixing her hair, as beautiful as an angel in her new dress. Going to the mustard tree at the foot of the hill, he sat down, prayed, and cried like a baby. Then he talked with God:

"Lord, isn't my love for Mary a far too human love? You know, Lord, I only want what is best for her. Yes, but I also want to be close to her and look at her and listen to her. O my God, she is the best fruit of Your creation!"

◆ ◆ ◆

Winter was mild that year. As it draws to an end, Uncle Ben is on the patio on a gusty clear day, selecting seed for the spring sowing. Ana is there at her embroidery. Mary is in her room, saying her prayers. It is midday. The wind drops, and the house sparrows grow quiet. God, always so close to this house, feels even closer today. An immense light appears in Mary's room. Uncle Ben thinks it's as if the sun were there. Ana stops working and observes attentively. Uncle Ben, sliding his seeds into the sack, is ready to go to Mary, but he does not move. Voices and mixed sounds are heard until shortly there is silence, so palpable it makes one shudder; the light gradually fades. In a while Mary comes out, her face flushed and exceedingly beautiful, her eyes moist. She slowly approaches her mother and embraces her. Ana kisses her and passes her fingers through her hair. Tears flow down Mary's cheeks. Finally she says:

"Mother, an angel has told me I am going to be the mother of the Messiah. I will have a Son by the Holy Spirit who will be called Jesus." She hides her face in her mother's lap.

Uncle Ben, still working, thinks: "Something has happened to this child, Mary. She is as beautiful as dawn and happy, but cries. She is her usual self yet does not seem the same. With her prayer she has brought closer to this house the light of God."

Some days later, Mary asks Uncle Ben to come with her on a walk to a tranquil spot, to the mustard tree. From this vantage point they can see the houses of Nazareth on the floor of the valley and, on the horizon, the distant mountains. Mary prays, meditates, and talks with God. After picking up branches and tying them with a string, Uncle Ben says: "Mary, my little one, is something wrong?"

"Prodigious things, Uncle Ben, that in time you will know about." She looks at him with exceeding tenderness, her gaze like a star that shines in the day.

Before spring, raptured and joyful, she asks him to accompany her to Ein Karem to visit her cousin Elizabeth who is expecting a child. Uncle Ben is delighted and moved: to accompany her, serve her, help her, listen to her voice and hear her laughter, watch over her sleep, mitigate her thirst and fatigue, defend her if needed with his own life. Uncle Ben mulled over the things they would take: the donkey's packsaddle, blankets, water skins; he would be as heavily loaded as the donkey, but who cares! In those days he worked harder than ever, and those nights he hardly slept, waiting for daylight.

For Uncle Ben the journey was a taste of heaven on earth; days spent walking next to Mary, watching her sleep under the stars. God was so close to them that he could see Him just by closing his eyes.

He enjoyed listening to Mary talk with the maidservant who also accompanied them. Sometimes she asked about the terrain they were crossing, of the animals or people they encountered. Everything seemed very beautiful to him: the stars in the night or the red clouds at dawn. He looked at her from the corner of his eye while lighting the fire, blowing on the logs, his eyes stinging. On the Sabbath, halfway there, Uncle Ben was moved when Mary fasted without speaking of it, with smiling dignity, busying herself with other things while he and the maid reluctantly ate something.

Mary, always helpful, didn't like to be served. She was the first to begin pitching or striking the tents; although she appeared delicate, she was not; she did these things to such perfection that Uncle Ben, an experienced and skillful man, was filled with admiration. At mid-afternoon, as the donkeys grew tired and the swallows flew low loudly twittering then rose toward the sky in swift pirouettes, Mary sang, accompanied timidly by the serving girl. Uncle Ben listened to her, enthralled, thanking God for those moments. Or he talked to them of God, telling stories from the Holy Scriptures or reciting Psalms. Afterward they prayed together until sundown.

Mary was anxious to get there, so they didn't stop in Jerusalem, not even to spend a more comfortable night in the home of relatives. In the evening, they reached Ein Karem and Elizabeth's house. Uncle Ben witnessed the meeting between Mary and her cousin as he unloaded the mounts. They hugged each other and then, to his surprise, Elizabeth fell on her knees and rested her head in Mary's lap; those watching fell silent, deeply moved. Then Uncle Ben heard Elizabeth's words, which left him perplexed and amazed: Mary, his little Mary, whom he had looked after since childhood, was being called blessed among all women. God had done something of great magnitude with Mary. And then he heard Mary's response, after embracing her cousin.

◆ ◆ ◆

Those months in Ein Karem were the happiest ever for Uncle Ben. As usual he worked as he was asked, now at the home of Zechariah, a big house with arable lands nearby. He accompanied Mary and Elizabeth whenever they went out to the orchard or the fields. He took his walks with Zechariah, a profoundly pious and wise man, now speechless. There was harmony and peace in this house, a home where God resided.

Mary and Elizabeth were always together, sewing or knitting garments for their future children, helping to store the harvests. Elizabeth became daily less able to do things, and her gait grew more awkward. She joked about her condition and age.

"Just like Sarah, Abraham's wife," she would say.

One day Elizabeth said to Uncle Ben:

"Ben, don't you know Mary is expecting a child? That infant is very special. He is the son of God Most High, the Messiah. We have been privileged to witness this marvel, and you to look after Mary from childhood. I am expecting a child who will be the precursor, he who the prophets foretold would prepare the way of the Lord, and Mary is the virgin who Isaiah said would be the mother of the Emmanuel, the savior of the world. And she is so modest, humble, and good, just as we have always known her. Don't tell anybody, Ben, not even Joseph. God has his ways."

From then on he looked upon Mary with even greater love. He was tempted to kneel when she walked by.

◆ ◆ ◆

Mary looked after the future mother and took care of everyone and everything. Her presence alone was enough to spread peace. Zechariah prayed and read, without being much involved in the running of the house. Uncle Ben helped wherever he was asked, making himself useful. The household became increasingly nervous as the birth of Elizabeth's child approached—the birth itself was a milestone, not only in the house but in the entire region. The wait was long and tense. Elizabeth was a strong woman, not a stranger to suffering, but already elderly.

At mid-afternoon of that mild day toward the end of summer, the midwives came. Zechariah, Uncle Ben, and some others sat about on benches or in the patio. The women kept coming and going. Mary appeared now and then. Time went by slowly, like the sun that slowly descended. Elizabeth moaned at times, then fell silent. At nightfall, by the light of a few oil lamps, the baby John was born in the arms of midwife who passed the infant to Mary, cleaned and wrapped in swaddling cloths. Upon hearing the first cry, those outside looked at each other and smiled. Mary soon came out with the child in her arms.

"Zechariah, this is your son, a beautiful boy. Elizabeth is well, just tired. Give thanks to God."

They looked closely at the child. Zechariah could barely contain his feelings. After three days, Elizabeth was up carrying the infant with Mary at her side.

As they were closing the gate the following night, Joachim unexpectedly appeared accompanied by a houseboy and two pack mules.

He was tired and covered with dust, but happy and serene as usual. When Mary heard of his arrival, she ran out to hug him with great joy. Uncle Ben joined in the greetings. Zechariah and Elizabeth received Joachim with great happiness and immediately showed him little John, whom Mary carefully brought from his cradle.

Joachim spent less than a week in that home, but those were days of intense love felt for each other. The good-byes were heartfelt. Uncle Ben sensed he would again see that family who had treated him so kindly. Joachim embraced Zechariah strongly and kissed Elizabeth, who, holding the little one in her arms, wanted him to carry away this image. Hiding her face under her shawl, Mary waved good-bye to her cousin.

On the homeward journey Uncle Ben was assailed by coughing fits at night and fatigue during the day. Mary prepared him herb drinks that he sipped like an obedient child while she watched to make sure he drank it all. Joachim joked with him about having the health of an ox and a long adventurous life. He had to make the last stretches of the journey mounted on the field hand's mule, wrapped in ponchos and with his legs hanging loose. Mary was by his side.

"Oh, Mary, how insignificant I am. You give fragrance to this field we are crossing, looking up at me, a poor, sick man. I am the one who should be looking after you and after that child you are expecting. My God, let it be that I might see him and hold him in my arms!"

Back in Nazareth, Uncle Ben sometimes was better and sometimes worse. He got up daily and worked as best he could. Ana scolded him and told him to look after himself, that he shouldn't be getting up yet.

"Woman, if to labor is my task, what would become of me with nothing to do? I'd be worse than my burro. It is fed because it works. Besides, this is how I can be with Mary and hear her voice and her laughter and be sure she does not strain herself. Ana, when will the birth be?"

"At the beginning of winter, Ben. And did you know Mary is to marry in a few days?"

Uncle Ben has often seen Joseph at the house. As soon as they returned from Ein Karem, he was there to see Mary. He came out serious and changed. He did not return for some days, then he came back, happy and smiling. Cleophas also came with his wife, Mary, as well as many other relatives and friends. One morning Mary said: "Uncle Ben, I am marrying Joseph. Will you help us ready the house next door?"

Work for Mary! That lifted his spirits and gave new strength to Uncle Ben. Even at night he would rise and go with the donkey to fetch sand from the river to mix with limestone. When he got back, Joseph, already working with a saw at the wood, greeted him with a smile and helped him unload. Uncle Ben raised some walls in the small house expertly made with big adobe bricks. With hands full, his clothing whitened by limestone, he worked ceaselessly, forgetting his cough, his leg, and his years. The houseboy helped him—a silent, prudent, selfless worker, simple in his gaze, a faithful man since youth.

At mid-morning, Mary would arrive with Ana, bringing something fragrant and steaming to eat. There was laughter in her eyes, a contagious happiness that made everybody smile and feel glad. Mary praised the progress of the work. Body and spirit refreshed, they kept on working. They labored into the night until the small house was finished: walls plastered, new floors of clay flagstone, strong wooden doors, windows reset, roof re-tiled, some beams replaced. The wedding of Mary and Joseph took place just four weeks later.

Once again Uncle Ben didn't want to be there. He left at dawn with the donkey to buy wool from shepherds on the other side of the mountain. It was to be his last outing from Nazareth. As the last guests were saying good-bye, Uncle Ben arrived, tired and dusty, and with a new fit of coughing.

Mary and Joseph moved into their new house, a patio's distance from Joachim and Ana's. Uncle Ben brought water to them daily, and visited with Mary, culling the wool he had bought. Autumn was gentle. It was still pleasant to be outside. Mary was happy. Joseph contemplated her, and Ana looked after her. Uncle Ben helped her however he could, bringing her the cut logs, clearing the weeds from the backyard, cleaning the pots neglected for years. How lovely was Mary in her youthful maternity! Women like that are more beautiful, more fulfilled, as if they had two souls.

He heard the talk about the herald but didn't pay it much attention until Mary, with a serious look, told him later that afternoon:

"Uncle Ben, we have to go to Bethlehem to be listed in the census. Would you look after the house until we come back?"

"But Mary, how can you undertake such a journey when you are about to have a child? Winter has begun. And the roads aren't safe. I'm going too."

"No, Uncle Ben, you stay here and look after that cough."

And when she gave him a hug, it seemed to him a tear rolled down her cheek.

"Look after yourself, Mary, my little one; take care."

"Uncle Ben, you know that God looks after me."

After they left, he guarded Mary and Joseph's house. He cleaned, swept, fed the chickens, amid the kitchen pots and pans and, in a corner, the little cradle they had prepared.

Time passes, but they didn't return. He knows the baby has been born and they are well in Bethlehem. Then one fateful morning Ana gives him the news.

"Mary, Joseph, and the child have had to flee to Egypt. Herod wants to kill the little one."

Uncle Ben falls silent. He goes to his room, to his corner, and stretched on his hard cot weeps with his hand covering his face.

"Oh Mary, my little one, what will become of you without my help on those desert roads! It would have been better had I gone with you despite this cough that has plagued me since autumn!"

Uncle Ben becomes quiet, hardly eats, works because, as he says, one has to work, but he retires early to his room. Ana cheers him up, tells him nothing will happen to them—God is with them.

One morning Ben doesn't get up. At times he coughs and then he sleeps fitfully. His look is vacant and often he mumbles: "Mary, my little one." Thus he spends the day and on into the night. Joachim and Ana keep vigil at his side, pray calmly, and look after him fondly. At dawn he seems to recover. He looks at everyone and thanks them; a few moments later, invoking God, he bows his head and dies serenely.

Arranging his pillows between sobs, Ana discovers a branch of thyme that Mary had left next to the baby's cradle.

4

$\mathcal{A}$ Light in the Darkness

"THERE ARE DAYS THAT DIVIDE HEAVEN from earth, and there are others that join them."

Winter is late in coming. Sparrows stir among their nests under the lower tiles. The wind hurries away some clouds to let the morning sun appear. Flapping its wings, a rooster crows while hens peck at the last grains from yesterday. Behind the door, Doggie barks at a passerby; Mary rises, gets ready in silence, and prays in the semidarkness of her room, unhurriedly, with faith. She feels so close to God that she forgets everything to focus on Him.

"Oh, my Lord, You who see and hear me, what do you want from me? I give You my soul, my youth, my life, all that I am, all that I have . . . is Yours."

Leaving her room she gathers her hair in a ribbon. Ana is already waiting, with a fire in the hearth. Her singing bird has begun to trill in its clean cage. Doggie comes close, barks happily, and jumps beside her. He is a mutt of indefinite breed, small, playful, and energetic. His snout is moist, and he has small eyes behind abundant hair. He is always eager to be with someone: Joachim on his way to the fields; Ana when she takes the bread out of the oven; Mary when she goes to the well in town or feeds the chicken, which he likes to scare. A loyal hound, he watches at night, barks at intruders, and hovers around friends, wagging his tail furiously.

Joaquin arrives and kisses Ana. The three peacefully eat a frugal breakfast.

Mary goes out to the patio. Fair weather promises, the breeze blows her hair, and she touches the first rosebud. She tosses grain to the chicken from a small basket, shooing away some intruding pigeons. Wood smoke from the neighboring chimneys is scattered about by the wind.

After a trip to the well, she places the jug on the cooling stone, and, taking up her needlework, goes to the patio of the little house next door that Joseph and Uncle Ben recently restored. It is separated from her only by a weathered adobe wall upon which vines and weeds have grown; it boasts the old fig tree at its center and, at the other end, a myrtle where turtledoves nest. The little house that formerly was used to store tools and grain from the harvests now looks clean and rejuvenated.

As so often before, she sits under the venerable tree, and, while sewing, thinks about all that has happened lately: her father, leaving his work in Jerusalem after so many years; her mother and her house; herself, her little room giving out to that narrow and noisy street, with a view of Mount Olivet. The years of learning and praying at the Temple. How many people from all parts of the world around her! The baaing of the sheep that went up terrorized to The Old Gate. . . . Now everything is so different: Nazareth is tranquil and provincial. She has new friends: Mary, who is married to Cleophas, her cousin. And she is betrothed to Joseph.

Joachim comes to say good-bye, and kisses her tenderly. He never tires of looking at his daughter: God must want something from her. . . . Never has he seen sulking, a complaint, a selfish whim, or useless vanity. In her, everything is clear, measured, illuminated, like her voice . . . and how he likes to hear that! Soft, melodious, a little grave; barely audible except when she laughs, like music that fills the air. My God, thank you that she was born to us in our old age, when against all hope I prayed with faith for her!

Joachim goes to his fields, followed by Doggie, who looks back to Mary, wanting simultaneously to go and to stay behind.

Outside, already saddled, is faithful Donkey. He peers curiously from the door toward the shadowy interior.

Since coming from Jerusalem, Joachim has concentrated on farming, and he has done well, being a careful, hard worker who attends to the present and looks to the future. The first harvest is already sprouting in his neat fields.

Uncle Ben comes to Mary and gives her a little bough bearing ripe lemons: "Here, these are the first ones of the year."

"Thank you, Uncle Ben."

Mary goes back to the house to help Ana with the housework. Pick up: there is a place for everything. Clean: a modest dwelling yet sparkling. Wash: she spends many hours at the wash tub bent over the clothes scrubbing and rinsing. How she likes the water! Even when she was a little girl she was glad of any excuse for getting wet in the stream while playing with her friends. "Mary of Cleophas is already expecting. What name will it be given?"

They hang up the clean clothes, pinning them securely to the line. The tiring morning chores—offered to God—are done. Mary has lunch with Ana, who today watches closely, thinking: *She is so beautiful, this daughter of mine! With her simple dress still damp in spots, sleeves rolled up, hair tied up in a ribbon, face flushed.*

"My daughter, your hands are red. You have been scouring too much."

"Mother, you always tell me that doing things right is more important than just getting them done."

Before noon, she goes to the little house next door. The new leaves of the fig tree give shade, the turtledoves flutter around their nest. Uncle Ben is working with his machete in a corner, observing her with a loving gaze.

Mary looks around her and sees something like a greater light that does not dazzle. The bleating sheep can be heard in the distance; a cicada sings in the heat. She goes to her room: simple, tidy, fresh-smelling. The bed is narrow; next to it is a small table upon which rests an oil lamp, together with the day's needlework. Through the small window with a worn wooden frame, one can see tile roofs, the valley, and the mountains that line the horizon. Mary sits on a whitewashed brick bench to say her prayers. She takes a roll of the Holy Scripture that Joachim lent her and meditates over a passage. Her mind and heart rise to God in an intense but unforced way; she talks and listens to Him; she loves Him and feels herself loved.

The sun reaches its zenith. There is no breeze. The birds fluttering in the eaves and Ana's singing bird all hush. Profound silence invades the house. Light fills Mary's room, and a bright and beautiful Angel stands before her. Mary is troubled at the exceedingly beautiful vision, but she attends and listens to him speak. His voice is like that of the men of her land. He utters that all the young women of Israel have for centuries wanted to hear. *Oh, the wonder of God's love for men! You have finally taken pity on them! How will this be? And her marriage to Joseph . . . ?* The answer is clear, sublime. The Angel himself is moved by it. Mary reflects, agrees, and places her life at the disposal of God.

The Angel vanishes, the light fades, and the room is brightened by the sunshine from the little window through which Mary stares.

"Oh, God of mine, You are in heaven and in my womb!"

Time passes, the sparrows resume their fluttering among the roof tiles, the bleating of the sheep is fainter, Ana's bird sings; a soft breeze stirs the leaves. God has come to his people and will remain forever.

❖ ❖ ❖

"Love dearly earned, doubly loved."

Joseph's strong hands work the jack plane back and forth over the rough wood. His thoughts are flying.

Mary—it has been more than three months since she left in haste. How is she? Mary, how much I think about you. The days without seeing you seem without light. My love for you grows, no matter the distance or not hearing your voice, however briefly, as the daylight wanes.

When it's time to stop working, Joseph picks up his tools, and he and the young man who is his helper clean up the wood shavings. The workshop is swept and straightened: angle irons hung up, saws in their places, wood laid flat so that it does not bend. They close up shop.

Joseph goes to Joachim's house. Ana greets him with a smile. She cares more for him every day, seeing in him the son she never had; she waits joyfully the marriage, for a grandchild she can hold in her arms and sing lullabies to, and for continuation of the line of David, now so diminished but from which the Messiah will come.

"Joseph, we have heard that Elizabeth has already had her child, a son. It is said that God's hand is upon him. Zechariah had been struck dumb. Joachim leaves for Ein Karem early. He will come back with Mary. He's preparing the beasts now."

Joseph goes to Joachim, who greets him happily.

"Joachim, I would like to go with you."

"No, Joseph, stay here taking care of Ana. She doesn't have anyone with her. You comfort her in Mary's absence."

They test Donkey's packsaddle. Fattened and stronger, he contentedly swishes his tail, sensing a journey soon. They bore a few more holes in the saddle girth. Joseph brushes him expertly and carefully.

"Donkey, you are lucky. Tomorrow you will leave for Ein Karem, and in a few days you will see Mary. You will hear her voice, you will bring her back. Behave well, Donkey—you are fortunate."

At dawn, Joachim leaves, accompanied by a field hand. Joseph gives him a basket of figs.

"May God be with you and the road rise up to meet you, Joachim."

"May God keep you, Joseph. Take care of Ana."

Days pass in quiet anticipation. On finishing his work, Joseph returns every afternoon to Joachim's house, where with great joy Doggie greets him, jumping around him, wagging his tail and barking happily. Joseph helps Ana bring in the chickens and load the bread oven so the bread will be ready at dawn. Later, while Ana sews, they chat: about the family, Jerusalem, Mary's childhood, the mountains of Bashan. Yesterday mingles with today and with tomorrows to come.

"You love her very much, Joseph, don't you? Yet you barely know her!"

"Ana, the time I have spent with her has been sufficient. Mary possesses something unique. It is not only her beauty, it is God's grace and charm that overflow. Sometimes I ask myself whether I shall be able to make her happy."

"Of course you will, Joseph. It is a matter of love, of work, listening with your head to your heart, living according to your means and loving the will of God."

"I work more, yet people pay so little. Sometimes I laugh and resign myself. At least I don't lose my sense of humor."

"God never abandons us, Joseph. You are just beginning."

Autumn comes, leaves fall, the corn ripens. Swallows come together in flocks to emigrate. Storks rise in majestic flight with their young until they are lost to sight. The afternoon freshens.

One day they are in the orchard when they hear Doggie barking. They go out and see the caravan approaching up the hill. Mary, riding Donkey, waves impatiently, her head covering billowing in the breeze. When they arrive Joseph helps Mary dismount. She allows him to kiss her hands, then blushes. As she leans on his arm, Joseph becomes aware of her thickened figure. They enter the house. In the warmth of the hearth, they speak of Elizabeth, of the infant John, of the journey and the happiness of being home. In the firelight, Joseph can clearly see that Mary is expecting a child. Ana observes and is silent. Joseph, distraught, mumbles a reason he must be going, says good-night, and leaves.

Joseph walks unsteadily, looking at the stars in the clear night sky.

"Lord God Almighty: What has happened? How can Mary most pure be expecting a child? She was away three months, could some act of unexpected brutality have been done to her on the way? Oh, Lord, give me light, light . . ." Tears drop from his eyes. Reaching home, he eats his supper and retires to his room. He cannot sleep. Hours go by. Far away cocks crow.

Bundled in her blanket, Mary warms herself by the fire in Ana's room. She can't sleep. "Mother, I am tired and I cannot sleep. I think Joseph realized my condition. What do I do . . . ? It's God's will; He will tell me. My happiness is such that I would like to share it with Joseph. What is he thinking?"

Tears spring from her beautiful eyes, reddened by weariness and the wind of the journey. It is serene weeping in which love and pain are mixed.

"Don't cry, my daughter. God has His ways. Everything will come right. God writes straight with crooked lines."

"My God, You know everything, You know how much I love You, and how much Joseph loves You. What to do? Do you wish, Lord, that I should tell him? Will he understand? This is so divine that no human words would suffice to tell it. Lord, You tell him, this is your Son. Oh, Joseph, will I see you again?"

Through the little window, she sees a small star amid the clouds, just like the tear that runs down her cheek.

Distant thunder announces a storm. The flames in the lamps flicker. Ana helps Mary lie down, tucks her in well, as when she was a little girl. Coming out, Ana hears Uncle Ben cough. He is wide awake.

Joseph wakes at dawn and listlessly prays: "God, You know everything. You know how much Mary loves You, and how much I do; and her parents and mine. What are we to do?"

He works all day in his workshop, his mind far away but without losing his good manners, because no one else is to blame for his uneasiness.

In the afternoon, he goes to Mary's house. At first he walks reluctantly, then he picks up his pace. Will she have an explanation?

Mary greets him as usual, serene, but with scarlet cheeks. On her lap, needlework. Doggie goes from one to the other, happily jumping. Joseph waits for the disclosure that never comes. The conversation is about family, harvest, rain. The opportunity is lost. Mary arrives with Cleophas, says happy and noisy hellos to both of them. Cleophas announces that they are going to have a child. Mary lowers her face over her needlework.

Joseph says good-bye although his brother protests. He throws a last glance at Mary, who looks at him sideways, her beautiful eyes now clouded.

Coming out into the cold night, he looks at the starry sky. "Oh, God, I cannot discredit her! That is impossible for me to do. I still love her intensely. I will leave her without accusing her, I want to go far away, for a while or forever. Oh, God, how difficult it is for me to do Your will. I judge not, nor do I condemn. I accept."

Those days he withdraws into his work from dawn to dusk. He doesn't go back to Mary's house. Doggie waits anxiously at the door, crying pitifully when he doesn't come.

Ana doesn't say a word. Mary prays. They work on the infant's clothing and blankets for the approaching winter. Joachim and Uncle Ben leave at dawn to harvest the late barley that they planted last summer. Donkey works vigorously, strong now and not tiring on the steep slopes or under the weight of the sacks.

Mary prays, watching at the door through which Joseph used to come.

"God in my womb! My bliss. Elizabeth called me blessed. How will this child be? Eyes as blue as heaven, his hair golden as wheat, skin white as the clouds. Oh, my son, you are not yet born and already you make me suffer! Thus my love for you is purified."

"Mary, wouldn't it be a good idea for to you explain everything to Joseph?"

"No, Mother, God knows best. He will tell us . . ."

Days have gone by that seem like months to Joseph. Work keeps him busy and his mind becomes serene, but the wound in his heart is still open. His parents observe him with worry. He is not the same. They respect his silence.

Joseph sleeps restlessly that night. Gusts of wind tell of coming rain. Then an angel appears to him in a dream and speaks to him clearly: He must receive Mary. The child she expects is the work of the Holy Spirit. Now he understands! Oh Mary, his Mary! Mother of the son of God! And he must marry her and care for that child. He prays until dawn.

When his parents see him in the morning, his demeanor is different. His eyes are bright as he explains to them: "I have decided to wed Mary as soon as possible. I hope her parents consent. It is not a year since we became betrothed."

"God bless you, Joseph. We are so happy with your decision."

The morning speeds by. The assistant is amazed to hear Joseph singing at work as he did months ago. Everything tidy, they close early and Joseph hurries to Joachim's house. At his loud knocking, Doggie barks joyfully. They greet him happily, Joseph tells Mary that he wants to talk to her. They move away from Ana and Joachim, so as not to be heard.

"Mary, an angel of the Lord spoke to me in a dream last night. He said this child you carry is the work of the Holy Spirit, and I must not fear to take you for my wife. Oh Mary, how happy I am! All my doubts have vanished. This son of yours will be the Messiah!"

Mary has listened eagerly, allowing Joseph take her hands and kneel before her.

"Joseph, my being proclaims the greatness of the Lord. I am still amazed."

"When do you want us to wed, Mary?"

"As soon as possible, Joseph. This child will be your son in the eyes of men."

"Oh, Mary, blessed are you!"

That day Joseph lingers in the house. They talk, make plans, look at each other in love. Outside it rains. When it clears, Joseph leaves. There is a smell of wet earth. A break appears in the clouds. The stars seem brighter tonight.

5

The Wind in the Crevices

IT'S WINTER. DOVES FLITTER DOWN to the patio where the sun is warm, and Mary feeds them beside the chickens. The shadows under the fig tree shrink. The wind spreads the scent of smoke from neighboring houses. Sometimes it is cloudy, other times sunny. Leaves rustle and then there is quiet. Within the house there is a sense of well-being. Mary and Joseph work in the brief hours of light, and then draw close to the fire.

Mary is still nimble. She is very young and bears her pregnancy well. Whenever Ana comes by—and that is often—she lovingly warns Mary to be careful. Mary smiles and works, welcomes her friends and relatives; her eyes shine with happiness and hope.

Joseph comes out to hear the town crier whom rumors from Jerusalem have anticipated. He greets Joachim, as usual working on his farming tools—"for springtime," he says winter after winter—and tells him he is going to the town square.

The imperial herald is clear and categorical, and Joseph is filled with apprehension: Quirinius, governor of Syria, orders everybody to register in a census. To have to go to Bethlehem, with Mary in her condition! He wants to ask questions; he seeks explanations. People crowd around, shout, talk, or fall silent. These are the whims of the powerful, little concerned with the inconveniences and afflictions of those who must obey.

Joseph returns thoughtful. He begs the Lord to enlighten his path: "What must I do?" Mary, unaware of this news, opens the door joyfully.

"Mary, we have to go to register in a census at Bethlehem, the city of David, our ancestor."

Mary doesn't say anything. She thinks of the trip, the cold, the bad weather, the unsafe roads, the child who soon will come. To leave the house, the cradle, the help of her parents, her friends and relatives. Where will the birth take place? Who will help? For the second time, she feels a sword piercing her soul. She remembers Micah's prophecy and exclaims to herself:

"My Lord, obeying this king, we obey You. How inscrutable are Your ways!"

She smiles at Joseph, her look tranquil, as if to say: the Lord knows best.

"When do we leave?"

"At dawn," says Joseph.

He goes out again to inform his relatives. Many are confused, some others have also decided to leave at daybreak, before the dry, brilliant days change to rain and sleet.

Mary goes to tell her parents she is leaving for Bethlehem. Ana has understood the will of God and dries a tear. How she would have loved to receive this child! Joachim promises to saddle the donkey and will improvise a place where Mary can sit safely. He too would be going except that he is no longer of an age for those journeys. God will provide.

Mary goes back to the house. Her eyes rest upon the cradle in her room made by Joseph's hands; the swaddling clothes still unfinished; that blanket a present from Mary of Cleophas, the little booties Uncle Ben knit. Joseph returns and they eat supper. Mary calmly talks about the journey, the roads, the possible companions; she knows it all well because she made this same trip just a few months ago. With admiration, Joseph quietly observes Mary. So young, so modest, so lovely, with that treasure in her womb. He has understood her commitment, and he says to himself: "Oh my God, look kindly upon me. Help me Lord. It is Your Son. Show me how to fulfill your will."

By the light of an oil lamp, Joseph goes to the workshop to pick up everything. In the house, Mary begins to put away what little they possess and can't carry with them. That poor donkey will have enough with her! The old chest fills up, with the help of Ana and her sister-in-law, Mary, who has arrived breathlessly with little James in her arms, to ask if they had heard the herald. Other friends and neighbors arrive. Mary and Joseph receive them and kindly say good-bye. Night falls, the chickens huddle together, the doves look on from the rafters. Ana and Joachim leave. Mary and Joseph pray together. The fire sputters in the hearth while the wind blows outside.

Joseph is up and about before dawn. Ana arrives and helps Mary get ready. She brings them something hot to eat.

"Daughter of mine, remember that God is in your womb, so how shall he not be in your path? Go in peace, and may his angels be at your side."

Joachim, well wrapped up, is already at the door. The donkey has been prepared. Uncle Ben finishes making the final adjustments to the packsaddle and seat and the provisions for the road. Donkey flicks his tail contentedly as though participating in the mystery his owners are living. When he exhales, he leaves a trail of breath visible in the uncertain light of dawn. When Mary leaves her mother's embrace, Joachim kisses his daughter tenderly, helps her mount, tucks her feet in. Uncle Ben, with tears in his eyes, holds the donkey. Joachim looks up at Mary. "Daughter of mine, may the Lord be with you, that my eyes may see the Messiah."

His words falter because he can say no more.

Deeply moved, Joseph takes hold of the donkey's reins and, lifting the ponchos and saddlebags to his shoulder, goes down the slope with a wave back. Mary's heart is pounding; the baby is moving in her womb. She turns to see the house, then, firmly settled in the seat, looks ahead over the rooftops of Nazareth. The red sun peaks between the mountains, lighting up the day.

Joseph's relatives are already waiting, and they join the boisterous and chattering group with their mules and donkeys.

❖ ❖ ❖

The journey will be long—five days at a regular pace. The landscape looks dry, the trees are leafless, no flowers in the meadows.
Donkey trots happily. He is so pleased to carry Mary! He cannot
go any faster, no matter how much he might want to, and seems
to realize that now his burden is more precious: Mary and the
baby she carries in her womb. God himself upon his coarse shoulders—what a great honor to be a beast of burden! He wishes his
pace were faster, his tread softer, his back more pliant . . . but
that's how he is, a tough donkey for so admirable a charge.

The prairie gives way to the mountain and sinuous footpaths.
The wind whistles on the crests, but is silent in the ravines, a silence
broken only by the murmur of the water in the winter streams rushing over stones. Sun and clouds above; stops along the way and tiring marches to the rhythm of the beasts. Animated conversations
and patches of silence become prayer and loving dialogue with God,
whom they perceive so close to His Son. Closer even than the column of smoke that accompanied His people through the desert.

The memory of her journey months back comes to Mary.
Then it was spring. How different the landscape is now, and how
different the circumstances! God in her life and in her being. Oh,
wonder of His merciful love! At last mankind will be redeemed
from that sin—human pride—that began with Eve. That world,
those fields she beholds, those people whom they encounter
along the way—all will be different. God has descended to the
earth. More and more Mary loves this world her Son will redeem.

Joseph hardly speaks. He looks at the road and watches her.
How good Joseph is! He never thinks of himself, never tires, is
always in a good mood, always solicitous. For him it is enough
to be aware of the Lord, of Mary, and to know himself loved.
Love is requited with love.

The nights are cold. Huddled around the bonfire, they eat
tranquilly, talk without raising their voices. A few words suffice

for them to understand each other. Their shelter is some wall or the courtyard of an inn. The stars blink up in the sky, seeming to want to come closer. The wind's whisper is like the flight of angels. Mary sleeps tired and serene under blankets; her heart rests in the Lord. Joseph dozes, vigilant even in sleep; he hears passersby and even jumps up when a stray dog approaches to sniff the sleepers. He wants something better than this for Mary.

"The poor don't have a roof at times, but they have the out-doors, they have the sky and horizons. We have You, Lord, and we will have Your Son."

Dawns are chilly, but the early morning rays of sun are com-forting. They have clean water from a stream, a frugal breakfast with hot spicy tea, while readying themselves for another day's journey. Donkey rests nearby, eating dew-laden grass, and has a long drink of water from the stream. Now he is ready to continue, for the way is clear, the direction sure, and the charge precious.

Mary feels the child within her and trembles.

"Will Donkey's trotting do him harm? Will he be born along the way? Will we reach Bethlehem? When will we return to Nazareth?"

Quails rise suddenly beside the road. Donkey is frightened. Joseph calls a halt at a place where the low hills open up to a ris-ing road. The sky is bright blue. The others also come to a stop.

"Are you well, Mary?"

"I would like to walk a little."

Joseph lends her his old walking stick, worn by roads and time, hand-carved of orange wood with a graceful staff formed patiently over a low fire. Donkey shudders and obediently fol-lows Joseph's footsteps.

Silence falls. Thus begins the soliloquy of souls with God. They pray and daydream. Soon after their fellow travelers pass by and continue on their way. Mary and Joseph remain alone. Donkey trots in the weak midday sun, hidden at times behind clouds. They stop for a bite to eat under some olive trees.

Donkey nibbles at some small bushes. Sheep at the foot of the hill are white dots against the brownish scenery.

Mary says, "Will we find lodging in Bethlehem? I feel as if the child will be born today."

Thoughtfully, Joseph, says, "God will provide. He is with us. Some good-hearted relative will take us in."

Carefully he cuts slices of bread and pieces of cheese that he gives to Mary: "Eat something. You need it."

Mary has hardly any appetite. She eats slowly. Her thoughts are centered in God; a tremendous joy invades her heart. She leans against a tree and takes a drink of wine mixed with water. How delicate Mary is, how beautiful, though tired and almost a mother! Mary looks at the twilight; from afar the houses of Bethlehem can be seen through the olive trees.

"Joseph, today could be the day of the Lord to be remembered by all generations: 'And you, Bethlehem, are not least among the cities of Judah, from you shall come a ruler, that will shepherd my people, Israel.' I would like you to cut me a little thyme to smell and take with me for when the child is born."

The sun goes down slowly as if wanting to contemplate the glory of this night. Mary again mounts the donkey after giving him a piece of bread. They begin the last part of their journey. The sun sets as they reach the first houses of Bethlehem. These are the last days of the census. Joseph heads for a relative's house not far off. A dog barks at them furiously at the middle of the street, and Donkey lays back his ears and gets ready to defend himself. Joseph intervenes and scares the dog off with a stick.

They arrive. They call; the response is slow; the door barely opens a slit. Joseph says who he is. The relative is not in the house. A voice is heard from inside: "We can't receive you. Look somewhere else, the house of another relative. . . ."

They go down alleys as it grows darker. People pass—some look at them; others don't notice them. Only the stars, beginning to twinkle in the firmament, seem aware that these men reject the Son of God. In another place, no room: the house is small, there are many, they cannot take care of Mary. They go toward the inn, where there are bonfires, voices, and laughter; the courtyard is full of people camping out and the porch is crowded. . . . Again they are on the street. A cold wind begins to blow. Mary's clothes swirl; the donkey lowers his head. The streets are dark. Joseph is becoming worried.

"Lord, where shall we go? It is Your Son who is to be born. Do not forsake us; we cannot go on like this, in this bad weather. It is for Mary that I suffer. I can withstand the harshness, Lord."

The road ends. They are at the edge of town: Where is this relative they've been told of? The donkey slips on the rough pavement and almost falls. Joseph grabs him on the edge of a ditch. They stop, and he hides his face in his sleeve to dry a tear on his weather-beaten face. Silently he prays; he does not know what to do. Mary is serene and quiet. Ahead lies the valley. The wind begins to blow harder, whipping sand into the travelers' faces. Farther on, a light flickers inside a house set back from the road. Dogs bark. A child wrapped in blankets up to his eyes comes near and stares at them in amazement.

"Don't you have anywhere to go? My father has a cave that shelters cattle."

As they approach the house, the boy calls, and his father comes out. They are poor, hardworking people, Joseph explains.

"If you want, come this way," the man tells them. "The place isn't very clean, but at least you won't be outside. My son will go with you. Son, take this oil lamp, and make sure the wind doesn't blow it out. And close the door well, so that the animals don't escape. My wife will come tomorrow to see you, missus. May God be with you."

The little boy with his lamp lights the stony path. Joseph firmly holds the reins of the donkey and stays close to Mary in case the beast stumbles. Scudding clouds speed across the crescent moon. They reach the cave that stands at the top of a slope. It is a desolate place, overgrown and filled with dry cattle dung. The old door closes only partially. The lad opens it, and in the sudden light of the oil lamp, the ox gazes with big eyes, and the mule kicks restlessly. There are mangers and loose hay.

Helped by Joseph, Mary dismounts. She can hardly stand up. She sits in a manger and looks about her. "Thank you, Lord! Here the wind does not blow. Blessed always be your will."

Joseph unloads the donkey, pats him fondly, and ties him in a corner with a handful of barley and a bunch of fresh hay. He spreads the blankets over some gear to dry. The boy brings wood from a corner and arranges adobe bricks as a hearth, then lights the straw and logs from the oil lamp. Now they have heat and light. Blessed fire, creature of God! Joseph gathers new straw, arranges the warm, dry covers in the cleanest spot, and helps Mary lie down, covering her with his mantle.

"Mary, are you well?"

"Joseph, I feel the child is ready to come."

The boy says he is leaving. Before he goes, Joseph asks where there is water.

"In front of the cave is a stream where they drink."

"Thank you, boy. Take this coin, and God bless you."

The young boy turns to Mary. "What is your name?"

"Mary."

"And you?"

"Joseph."

"My name is Judas. Good-bye."

Joseph goes out with him to get water. The weather has calmed; the wind has dropped. Only the cold remains, a reminder that it is winter.

He gives water to Mary and drinks himself, then fills the donkey's pail and puts what is left on the fire to boil in a small earthen pot brought from Nazareth. He settles down near Mary and takes out something to eat. She does not want any. Her lips are moving in prayer.

"Lord, should I find a midwife? But where? And leave Mary alone? I should not have let the boy go. Oh my God, see the place where Your Son is to be born, poorer than a fugitive slave. My Lord, I feel guilty."

Close to midnight Mary quivers. "My God, help me! I feel Your presence so close I can almost touch You."

A great silence invades the cave. The light from the fire flickers. Joseph takes the boiling water and a knife with blade reddened by the fire. Then there is a baby's cry.

"Oh, Mary, Mary, he is born! Do you feel pain?"

"No, Joseph, it's like a ray of sunshine."

Joseph takes the child.

"Let me wash him. How beautiful he is! Almighty God, blessed be Your Son that You have brought into the world!" He cannot keep back his tears of joy and sorrow, love and happiness.

"Look, Donkey, this is Jesus. How small and defenseless! A crying child who is Lord of the universe!"

He washes and dries the infant and kisses him.

"Take him, Mary. How beautiful he is!" Mary cradles him and holds him close to her, looking at him tenderly.

"My son and my God." Her tears of love fall on him.

Joseph steps outside to dispose of the water. The night is cold and serene, with a star-studded sky. Shining on the eastern horizon is a new star he has never seen before. He throws more branches on the fire, tucks in Mary, arranges Donkey's packsaddle as a pillow, and lets her rest. He wraps himself in his blanket in front of the fire, but despite his fatigue he cannot sleep. It is all so remarkable! Later that night, seeing that Mary cannot sleep for holding the child, Joseph rises and takes him, well wrapped in swaddling clothes, to a manger where with great care Joseph places him upon the straw. The child sleeps. Joseph keeps vigil nearby.

Then there are voices outside, faces at the door, knocking. Joseph gets up to find shepherds. In their coarse dialect they tell of angels, a light in the sky, singing. Entering, they come close, the fire illuminating their weathered faces, beards, and disheveled hair. In their rough hands they bring gifts to the child. Mary lifts the covers and lets them see the baby's head. They stare in silence, in the flickering light of the fire.

"This is the child! God with us. Blessed be the Lord!"

They leave thoughtful but happy. A dog that came with them carries off a half-eaten piece of bread Joseph had left. And he, exhausted, finally sleeps. Mary, eyes fixed on the manger, rests and ponders these things in her heart. The last flames die to embers. The angels keep watch; the bright star of the East is now in the sky above.

6

The Rainbow

JOSEPH WAKES WITH SUNLIGHT IN the stable. Mary, with the child in her lap, combs her hair silently while dialoguing with God. Joseph takes the baby and holds him tenderly, fondles and kisses him. "How small he is and how beautiful!" Then he returns him to his mother.

He goes outside. The morning is cold and calm, but the sunlight is warm. He takes the donkey to drink and forage very happily and leaves him unfettered. When he returns, he meets the boy and his mother coming with something warm to eat. They approach Mary, who smilingly shows them the child.

Joseph goes out to search for lodgings in the town, leaving his wife and child, now sleeping, with that good woman, who lovingly shares with Mary her experience as a mother. Simon, the lad's father, welcomes Joseph and is astonished at the birth of the child. He knows what the shepherds have said and wished to see the child as soon as he could.

"Why are you going to call him Jesus? Is there someone with that name in your family?"

Joseph simply says "That is what he must be called."

They talk about the place and its customs, drinking strong, sweet tea while they dunk a soft meal bread the daughter brings them. Simon tosses crumbs to the doves swirling beside him.

Chatting bonds them, and they become friends. Joseph explains his need for a place to stay.

"A house or a room nearby? I know of one that belongs to a good friend who rents rooms not very far from here. I'll go with you to see him."

They go out. The day is splendid, the sky clear and cloudless, the air pure, nature clad in austere beauty. People smile at one another when they greet. The house shown to them has two rooms for rent, with a shared courtyard with a fountain where children play. They talk, bargain, agree. Joseph goes happily back to the shelter. The stream shines in the sun, the mule and the donkey quietly forage nearby. The lad opens the door when he arrives. Sunlight enters with him, illuminating the face of the child, eyes open and questioning like his mother's. Joseph thinks, *These are the windows through which God is looking at this world of ours.*

Soon neighbors start to arrive. They have heard the news carried by the shepherds. These are field hands and townspeople, shepherds, and shopkeepers. Mary, happy and amazed, does not tire of showing them the child. Joseph answers their questions, thanks them for coming, and says good-bye as they go on their way.

They spend the day in the sparsely furnished rented house. Joseph soon finds work in a small carpentry workshop nearby. The pay is little, but it helps. Registering for the census is prolonged. Winter is coming, it is not a time for traveling. They must stay in Bethlehem.

The child grows by leaps and bounds. Now he can move his head and hands together. Mary recovers and works at the house. The donkey stays in the cave with the mule and the ox. He is happy he was the first to see the child and sad at not seeing him now or hearing Mary say: "Come on, Donkey, come on, and don't look back!"

They live in impoverished dignity. The earthen floor, covered in part by some braided reed mats Joseph has obtained, gives warmth to the room. There are a pair of chairs and a formerly rickety table bequeathed to them by some neighbors, that Joseph has made good as new. Crude cooking pots and pans are kept spick-and-span as beaten gold by Mary. They have ceramic plates bought from street vendors and a glazed jar with a curved handle resembling the neck of a heron purchased for a few extra coins. The hearth, fastened to the central wall where Mary cooks, heats the quarters and Joseph's hands when he comes back from work, as well as the face of the child that reddens in the firelight. Mary knows how to use even the most ordinary things and takes advantage of everything, her hands move skillfully and to perfection; she stretches every penny and prepares simple fare, filled at the same time with so much love for God that Joseph is amazed every day.

Eight days after the birth they must take the child to be circumcised like all males in the line of Abraham. The task of implanting the sign of the divine alliance upon the flesh of his child—the one through whose blood this alliance has been established—rests upon the shoulders of Joseph as head of the family. But Joseph prefers that it be done by an expert and pious elder whose services parents in this place customarily employ.

In the evening, having cleaned up from work and changed his clothes, Joseph gathers the ten witnesses, whose presence guarantees the child's incorporation into the chosen people. Joseph holds the child, Mary the white cotton cloth. The knife cuts, the child cries, the first divine blood is shed. The rabbi repeats: "Blessed be Jehovah, the Lord. He has sanctified his beloved from the womb of his mother and has stamped his law on our flesh." Mary whispers:

"It's over, my son. This is how it had to be. Child, like the rest of your people, man among men."

She hugs him and covers him in kisses. Before the witnesses and the scribe holding the awl and the tablet, Joseph clearly pronounces:

"His name is Jesus, son of Joseph, of the tribe of Judah, from the lineage of David, born in Bethlehem."

◆ ◆ ◆

Jesus grows. Now he looks at people with lively and gentle eyes. He grasps Joseph's strong finger in his hand. He is a healthy child, sleeping in the embrace of the sunlight while Mary sews, irons in silence, or washes at the basin with cold water that reddens her most pure hands. She prays at work. When people visit, she talks of God and small daily events with the neighbors. She listens attentively to them and soon makes herself beloved for the love that flows from her as from an overflowing vessel.

Townspeople and others living in the vicinity have come to see the child, drawn by the shepherds' news. Some are awed by his beauty and that of his mother; others admire the simplicity with which they live, and others—fewer—just looking on the child and listening to Mary, are filled with joy and hope for the arrival of the Messiah.

Mary receives them kindly and attentively. Only God knows how difficult it sometimes is for her to be interrupted in her intimacy with him. Among those who come are some who bring something for the house or food. Joseph, tired after work, must say a friendly good-bye to the inquisitive ones.

Forty days have passed since the birth of the child. It is time to go to Jerusalem to fulfill the dual requirement of Mosaic law: legal purification of the mother and presentation of the child at the Temple.

"Mary, you don't need to go."

"Joseph, I will go like any other woman of my people. Get the donkey, and let us go."

It is Saturday. The morning is unpleasant and cold. Donkey, close to the cave, brays happily. Joseph pats him and brushes him, cleans him and puts the packsaddle on him. Donkey is glad to have work to do at last. As they pass by the house of their friend Simon, he greets them cordially. The boy puts fresh baked bread in the saddle bag. With the food still hot in a little basket and the child well wrapped in her mantle, Mary gives the donkey a pat and rides on.

The road to Jerusalem is always traveled by farmers on their way to sell their produce, shepherds with their flocks, peasants, traders, and pilgrims. Mary and Joseph do not attract attention. Mary hides her singular beauty under an ample veil. But aware of what he is carrying, Donkey's gait becomes a happy prance.

At mid-morning they reach in Jerusalem, the Holy City, worldly, wealthy, and full of misery, yet beloved of God among all the cities of the earth. They ascend Mount Moriah toward the Temple. Mary is joyful at submitting herself to the will of God, manifested to men in his laws, by presenting her firstborn to Jehovah. Joseph is serene, with the profound joy of a holy man who not only goes to the Temple of his God but does so accompanying two creatures so dear to the Lord.

Leaving Donkey outside, they go to the courtyard of the Gentiles. It is crowded at this hour with vendors and money changers in their places and visitors and pilgrims coming and going. They buy the two turtledoves for the sacrifice. Soon a venerable old man approaches and, gazing at them with deep and shining eyes, and asks to hold the child in his arms. Mary is surprised and looks at Joseph. Joseph, moved, assents. The child awakens and Mary gives him to Simeon. Tears rolling down his wrinkled face, he praises God. Mary and Joseph are amazed. Simeon returns the child gratefully and blesses them with great affection. Then he addresses Mary: "A sword shall pierce your soul. . . ." Now Anna comes, elderly and dignified. Observing the child intently, she breaks into jubilant exclamations, touches him, kisses him. Praising God, she speaks of the child to everyone who has come to see what she is exclaiming about.

Mary and Joseph cross the courtyard. Passing the stone balustrade that marks the limit of access permitted to pagans, they climb some steps and cross to the Beautiful Gate beyond which lies the stairway to the Gate of Nicanor, decorated with gold and silver, that leads to the Courtyard of the Israelites. Here Mary and Joseph stop humbly, along with other couples come to ransom their firstborn as prescribed by the Law.

Still thinking of the prophecy of Simeon, Mary holds the child even closer to her breast. Slowly they go in turn up the stairs. When they reach the top, the priest takes the two pigeons that Mary offers, asking his prayers for her and that one be offered to reach purification and the other in gratitude to God for the son He has given her. Taking the child from Joseph's arms, she presents him while Joseph gives the offering for the ransom. Then they move away to make room for others.

Having done what they came to the Temple for, they greet some of Mary's relatives and share food with them from what they are carrying and from what is offered to them.

The child has fallen asleep, arms outstretched, defenseless, upon a great bed. He is admired by everybody. In the afternoon, they begin their return to Bethlehem. Donkey has eaten a few handfuls of barley given him by Joseph and drunk deeply from a fountain at the house. He is happy at again carrying the sweet weight of Mary and the child and hearing her say:

"Come on, Donkey, not much farther."

Saying good-bye to the kind family, they tell them that in a few weeks, when the weather improves, they will go back to Nazareth.

As they are on the road, a cold wind rises. Daylight is fading as they reach the town's first houses. Looking to the horizon, Mary sees the new star that shines more brightly than the rest. Is this the star of her son? It's a fresh omen of pain—the sword that Simeon foretold.

Now it is back to work. Joseph labors in the workshop at a job thankless and harsh in winter, extending from dawn to dusk and badly paid. He offers each hour, each hammer blow, each plank sawed to God, in a contemplative and silent dialogue. Because clients find him amiable and reliable, the workshop thrives, but the pay is very little. The owner insists he cannot afford more and resents even the shavings and slivers that Joseph takes home, but he says nothing and does not meet his gaze. It is to his advantage to have Joseph there.

Mary's heart is filled with joy at seeing the child so healthy and beautiful. She sews clothes that the neighbors bring her—how glad she is for the hours spent learning from her mother in the courtyard in Nazareth! She irons with an old borrowed iron heated over the red embers on a small, dilapidated brazier. She works quickly and well; her thoughts fly to God and her gaze to the child.

One afternoon there is bustle in town. A caravan with horses and camels has arrived, picturesque and strange. These are important people from foreign lands: three lords on their mounts together with servants and beasts of burden. They ask for the child-king born more than forty days ago. They have been directed to the house of Joseph and Mary by the shepherds. People accompany them to the very door of the house. The courtyard is crowded with the Magi and their baggage, neighbors, and curious onlookers.

Joseph has just returned from work. Alarmed and still in his work clothes, he comes outside while Mary takes the child in her arms. Here is another omen! The strangers humbly approach. Seeing Mary's loveliness and simplicity and Joseph's bearing, they have no doubt that the star has brought them to the Son of God.

"Is this the child?"

Joseph nods. Mary shows Jesus to them. They observe him intently, kneel before him, and adore him. The neighbors and onlookers fall silent, engrossed; servants and unseen angels are speechless. The Magi represent all men of good will. The Savior of the world has come, and they behold Him. Taking out gifts, they place them before the child. Mary sits down and offers them a seat; the fire is rekindled, and their weather-beaten faces are illuminated. Asked where they come from and how they found this house, they say: "We saw his star above us."

Joseph understands. Looking up, he sees the star, new and brilliant. Mary's heart swells. Now it is not only shepherds and neighbors. People from far away also know the Son of God has been born.

She hands them the child whom they look upon with tenderness, slowly passing him from one to the other. They kiss him with tears in their tired eyes. The journey was worth it, leaving everything they owned, the uncertainty of the road and destination. This was their purpose in life: to reach the Son of God. And, lo, it is he that they now hold. Happily they produce food and share it. Joseph offers them water and a jug of wine. Mary keeps the child close by. Night falls, and they retire to their tents to rest, taking one last glance at the child asleep in his cradle before they leave.

7

The Footprints of God

It is several hours since the departure of those good Magi from afar. The amazement and curiosity of the local people have passed; all is calm again. In the small house the presence of the Magi lingers—their appearance, their tenderness with the child, their love for the God whom they hardly know. The Magi hardly tasted food while there and spent only a few hours before leaving, well into the night, more to let Mary rest than because they wished to cease gazing on the child, holding him, kissing him. They departed suddenly, quickly preparing their beasts and, after embracing Joseph and giving the sleeping child one last glance, hastily set out. Joseph sleeps restlessly now. And then God speaks to him clearly. It is not a dream. He rises urgently and wakes Mary.

"We must leave right now; we must flee. Herod wants to kill the child. God has shown me this while I slept. This is why the Magi left so soon."

Mary lifts the child and holds him close, while dark forebodings cross her mind. Then she rises, and by the light of the rekindled hearth she starts to collect the few things they can carry with them. Carrying an oil lamp, Joseph goes to rouse Donkey. The dogs bark, and the landlord pokes his head out. Mary tells him they are leaving, heartily thanks him for the days they spent in the house, and pays him. She leaves everything tidy and clean. Joseph, a pained look on his face, appears with Donkey who, already prepared, snorts in the cold. He is an uncomplaining burro, always at the ready, never budging until summoned. He seems constantly eager to look with moist eyes at the child Mary now wraps in her shawl.

They say good-bye to the neighbors who have appeared, curious and wondering. As they enter the dark alley, a frightened dog barks. Intense cold sharpens their sleeplessness and fear. The narrow, empty road ends abruptly, and various ways open up before them. Joseph sets off firmly toward the mountains visible in the moonlight. The bright star first seen at the birth of Jesus is no longer to be seen. He must take the road south, toward Egypt and away from Herod's soldiers.

Dawn breaks. The earth is hard and wet. The donkey stumbles going up a steep climb. Mary, silent, meditates in her heart and prays.

"Lord, I carry your Son, the one whom You placed in my womb, he who comes to save mankind. That king does not love him, but why should he wish to take his life—this little piece of heaven and flesh whose heart beats beside me and who feeds from my breast? Oh God, how incomprehensible are Your ways!

From the top of the hill Bethlehem can be seen sleeping in the light of early dawn. Riders approach along the road from Jerusalem.

The morning is cold. The journey grows wearying as the hours pass. Joseph walks rapidly in front, seeming to drag the donkey. He can imagine the sound of galloping horses behind him, followed by the cries of the child as a sword pierces him. No stopping now. They bypass Hebron. The dialogue with God continues and gives strength and serenity. Past midday they stop to eat something and let the donkey rest. Mary can hardly hold herself upright. She is numb. The child looks about and seems to smile. They rest in the shelter of a mud wall. When someone goes by, Mary covers herself and the child. Joseph looks away distractedly.

Some wayfarers driving mules and donkeys laden with firewood approach slowly. Joseph steps out to greet them and wishes them peace.

"Where are you going?"

"Toward Gaza by the sea."

They appear to be decent, hardworking woodcutters from the neighboring mountains. "May we join you?"

The men consult one another. Their hearts soften at seeing Mary, so young, and the child, so small.

"Come with us."

Mary and Joseph feel heartfelt thanks to God. They walk together a long way until at last they stop to set up camp at the edge of a stream under the shelter of a few carob trees. Soon they are resting beside the blaze the woodcutters have set.

Another day dawns. The caravan gets ready to move on. While Mary prepares something to eat, Joseph holds the baby.

"How tiny he is, and how beautiful! His little hands are perfect. Oh God, marvelous is all Your creation, from flowers to stars, but so much more this son! He is Your Son and, according to the Law, mine. I registered you in Bethlehem, child, in that ancient scroll with so many names of kings and carpenters, putting down the name Jesus. Jesus—that is how the angel named you, that is your name, and that is the name by which I love you."

Donkey is ready. He has nibbled the grasses by the stream and during the night rested in preparation for another day's journey like yesterday's. The travelers are less anxious; Herod is farther away.

At mid-morning, Mary tells Joseph she wants to walk until the sun grows strong and asks him to carry the child. And thus they walk along those increasingly arid paths that herald the desert ahead. When they reach Beersheba, the last town of Palestine, they say good-bye to the woodcutters.

"God be with you," Joseph calls out to them.

They search those dusty, scorched streets for a place to buy provisions for the road: flour, cheese, salt, dates, honey, carob beans, and barley for the donkey. They are poor and don't ask for much, but Joseph is worried. Does Mary need milk? What wouldn't he give to be able to lay the whole world at the child's feet! He dares not display the Magi's gold, lest the gold and their lives both be at risk.

They rest in the town square like other travelers, under the shade of trees. Dust, clay, and limestone are the stuff of this town on the edge of the desert where a few springs supply the water for anything to live there and for the town itself to be a last green spot before the burning sands. They stare in alarm at every passing horseman, still wary of the menace of Herod. They are frightened when soldiers come by; but the men regard these poor, dust-covered individuals with indifference.

Soon a large caravan with camels and asses arrives. The beasts crowd together. Children play, men talk, women silently prepare food. Poverty and friendship, dirt and cleanliness of a sort, generosity and selfishness mingle in a common struggle against the harshness of the desert.

Joseph approaches the men who seem to be leaders.

"Where are you going?"

"Toward Egypt."

Good news! Joseph tells them he is looking for work there where some relatives live. He travels with Mary and the child in swaddling clothes. They will be no trouble.

Questions, answers, uncertainty. Besides being guides, they will provide food and water. A price is agreed upon. Joseph is invited to drink strong hot tea with them. They will set out at dawn, traveling the sea route.

The moon lights up the square. The bonfires die to embers. The tired donkey falls asleep, as the child has done long since. Mary and Joseph pray.

The caravan starts under a sun that has been blazing since it rose. Where there is water, the landscape is beautiful. At the last spring, close to the last clump of houses in Judea, the men eat and the beasts drink until filled, as if knowing what lies ahead. Water skins replenished, the march is resumed.

The road becomes a footpath. Vegetation is scarce. The caravan forms a single file; the pace of the animals becomes rhythmic and slow. The people are silent, except for one who says to Joseph, "We have passed Idumea."

Mary hears and is grateful. They are beyond the reach of Herod's cruel power.

The sun is relentless. Before them, dunes, shorn hillocks, and sand; behind them, the green mountains of Palestine, azure in the distance. Mary thinks of Beersheba, Jerusalem, and Nazareth, where Joachim and Ana wait. How they will suffer at not hearing from them! The caravan halts at the foot of low hills where there are caves in which they take shelter for the night. Evening falls and refreshes. Again the bonfires, the conversations, the children's games. Donkey is thirsty. Joseph gives him a small amount of water. Seeing a mound of soft sand nearby, the beast throws itself on it and rolls happily in it, stretching and bending his legs. Then, rising, he shakes himself and is quiet. Mary cannot help smiling.

"Jesus, see what Donkey is doing. Silly Donkey! But good Donkey."

Mary lets of the beast lick salt from her hand.

It is still dark when they rise. The cold is intense at first, but soon there is sultry heat. The caravan advances slowly and steadily, with Mary and Joseph toward the rear. Past noon there is a halt in the march. Joseph prepares the ground with his mantle and pitches an improvised open tent, using their blankets for shade. Mary rests there, gazing upon the faraway mountains. Joseph gives her water and holds the child on his lap, shielding him from the sun. "How fair to behold! He has Mary's eyes. His mouth is small and sweet. His perfect hands grasp my big, calloused ones. This is the Son of God! Help us Lord, this heat is exhausting. Mary is tired, and it is only the second day of the five or six the journey will last!" Joseph nods. He wakes when the baby cries and passes him to his watchful mother.

The sun sets in the west. The temperature plummets. They cluster together. "Will the donkey's hoofs withstand the burning sand?" Joseph prays they will. "What a small thing, though so important, to ask of God!" The caravan resumes its course toward the red sun slowly setting over the sea of sand. As night begins, they stop again, next to some palms and a well with salty water—maybe the last water before Egypt. Mary prepares food that Joseph takes from the bag he has carried on his shoulders the whole time. He unloads the donkey and gives him two measures of barley and something to drink. The child wakes in the firelight and laughs. Mary brightens and laughs with him. Joseph cuts the little amount of wood that they have carried; tomorrow there will not be even this much.

Fellow travelers from the caravan come to talk with them. The women admire the child. "Why so young and beautiful—and in this desert? What has happened to bring them here?" They are accustomed to the dust, to the hot sand that the wind blows in their faces, to nights in the open air. But Mary is not; her face is reddened from the sun. "Poor woman!" Mary, beloved of God.

They ask when the child was born and where. Not so long ago, yet it seems so remote. "How far away Nazareth and Bethlehem seem, and the shepherds and the star, far more brilliant than these along the horizon behind the dunes!"

The night passes. Another day's journey begins. Mary and the child mount the donkey, which switches its tail contentedly, even though he hasn't had much to eat. This is a beast of burden whose job is to walk carrying its charge. Joseph tightens his knapsack under his shoulders and adjusts the turban upon his forehead. The caravan moves out in the early morning freshness. Their shadows lengthen on the sand. Mary and Joseph raise their thoughts to God and pray in silence while the people around them laugh and speak in their picturesque tongue. Now the sun is high. Everyone becomes quiet, the beasts continue their pace, the baby falls asleep. Joseph asks himself, "How far will we get today?" Mary wonders, "When will we stop?" She shelters the child in her robes. The sight of him consoles her.

At noon they stop again. There is no shade now. Only sand, stones, dust footprints left by other caravans passing this way over the centuries. Helped by Joseph, Mary dismounts with difficulty. She rests under a tent he prepares for her. The sun is blazing. There is no explaining the will of God, but He is very close. Angels also look on. The earth hushes. Donkey lowers his head and eats, keeping her company while Joseph goes for water. Mary bends forward and pets him as she removes his reins.

Donkey, what more could you want? God's mother has stroked you, and that makes anything else worth the trouble. Joseph returns with water. They drink slowly; with a wet cloth he refreshes his wife's temples. A little girl from the caravan approaches with a wooden bowl of milk that she gives to Mary. She remains gazing at the Queen of Heaven—now a weak traveler—with large and sad dark eyes. "Do your lips hurt?" she asks in her nomad tongue. Mary looks at the child, who kisses her hand and leaves.

The journey resumes. Night falls and, with it, the cold. Mary shivers, but at the same time she smiles and is tranquil. After a meager supper, eaten in silence, they wrap themselves in their mantles together with the child and watch the big stars lighting the sky. The child occasionally cries, and she worries about him, but she knows well that God will not abandon them. They will reach Egypt because the Angel has said so.

"But what a heavy burden, Lord—this hasty flight from Herod! This is how so many have suffered and will suffer yet down through the centuries from cruel and capricious tyrants who inflict suffering on people—even defenseless children like this one in my arms—to promote their own interests. Lord, this is only a trial. As gold is refined in a crucible to be purified, so are we tried so as to deserve this child."

Joseph brings more wood. The embers illuminate his tired face and reddened eyes, but he is always serene, strong, and vigilant. He lays himself at Mary's feet and falls asleep. Mary covers him and prays until she also sleeps.

Day breaks. The harsh, monotonous trek continues. Their path crosses that of other caravans. Dogs bark, strangers greet one another like friends; the road bonds them. People look at Mary with amazement, and at Donkey, and at Joseph. "Why on earth did they venture into these sands without better mounts?"

Another leg of the trip, and another, and yet another. On the fifth day, past noon, they rest in a hollow. The caravan halts not far ahead. Mary can hardly hold herself upright on the donkey. Joseph helps her dismount and sit under the scarce shade of the blankets. He gives her water and looks at the half-asleep baby. The wind rises, blowing dust that blinds the eyes. Joseph fastens the stakes of the tent in the sand; Donkey, frightened, flees. The wind increases and the sun darkens. Joseph gets under the tent and protects Mary, who covers the child. They turn their backs to the wind, now becoming a fierce sandstorm. As the minutes go by, they can hardly breathe; the dust is covering them. They pray; God is near. The angels contemplate them silently. Joseph recites Psalm 2.

The wind dies down. Now there are only gusts, and then all is silent. The sun is visible once more. Joseph shakes off the sand, rises, and helps Mary. They take a few steps and from a height observe—nothing. The caravan is gone and so is Donkey. Only sand and sun. Joseph goes to collect the blankets, the stakes, the half-empty knapsack and the skins with a sip of water still in them.

He takes the child from Mary, letting her hold his knapsack, and they begin to walk to the west, slowly, trusting in God, who will not abandon them, because this child is His Son and He loves them. Their footsteps are making a new path on the soft sands. Step after step their strength seems to ebb. Then there is a dot in the distance, something dark on the white sands. It grows more and more visible. It's Donkey! He is alone, still half-covered in sand. In a moment of panic he fled like a coward, thinking only of himself, his life, his liberty. He ran away and he kept trotting until the wind stopped. And the child? And Mary? And Joseph's anguish at being abandoned? These are the people he loves. Where are they? He is still and sad; he has lost them! But then he hears steps and voices close at hand.

"Donkey! Thanks be to God!" He feels Joseph's strong hand on his flank. Joseph brushes away the sand, and Mary's sweet voice says:

"Donkey, what happened to you?"

The poor burro lowers its head even more while Joseph helps Mary mount it. But Donkey doesn't walk. His headlong flight has left him exhausted, eyes glassy and tongue dry. He tries to take a step forward and simply can't. He cannot carry Mary, sweet weight that she is. If only he could cry in rage and shame for his cowardice! Mary dismounts and walks behind Joseph, who carries the baby beside Donkey, grasping him with one hand on the packsaddle. The sun beats down. Their steps become slower, heavier. They are thirsty; they stare straight ahead. Joseph carries the infant on one arm, the knapsacks on the other. Weariness grips him. His steps become uneven and he drags his feet. Worried for the child, he continually gives him water. At times the infant cries and other times he sleeps. How long can they go without food? How strong Mary is! She is dragging herself more than walking, but not a single complaint escapes her.

Suddenly a whiff of humid air smelling of the sea!

"Mary, the sea isn't far. God be praised!"

Before them objects grow larger as they approach them. Palm trees and animals and men: the caravan!

Joseph helps Mary walk the last stretch, resting one hand on her shoulder and the other on the donkey. Feeling the sea breeze on its dry skin, the beast starts walking faster. The sun sets over the sea, spreading crimson across the water. They reach the palm trees. This is a small oasis a short distance from a sea whose soft silver waves are flecked with foam. They rest under the shadow of some junipers. People from the caravan approach with fresh water and dates.

"Praise God, you arrived. We came this far to avoid the wind, the sand, the sirocco."

The little girl approaches Mary with her milk gourd.

"Take, lady. For you and for the baby"—whom Mary tenderly feeds on her lap.

Joseph gives water to the donkey, as much as he wants. He unsaddles him and lets him go free.

"Poor Donkey, he is half blind. If he had stayed with us when the wind came, I would have covered his head."

Before sundown they go close to the water's edge. Donkey follows behind, limping. Joseph sees that his hoofs are bleeding. He rolls up his robe and lets the waves wet his feet. Mary does the same. They splash water on their reddened, dusty faces. Joseph manages to bring Donkey to the water, but he is frightened and bucks. The salt irritates his wounds and tears seem to spring to his clouded eyes. Mary bathes the child with water that she pours gently over his small body.

They sit on the seashore to dry off; a sea curlew with its long beak hunts clams, darting to and from the waves; both of them laugh. It has been so long since they could do that! Mary lifts Jesus and turns him toward the sea.

"Look, son of mine, the big sea, immense and so beautiful. Way over there, on the other side, are many people, and cities and lands, all created by God the Father for you." And her prayers flow serenely while the sun drops below the horizon. They put on their sandals and return to the camp.

They rest with the caravan all day and make more friends among these coarse, boisterous, selfish people, who nevertheless are in their own way kind. For their part, their companions marvel at this poor couple who express no complaint or grievance, pray continuously to their God, and care for the child as their most precious treasure. At daybreak they all move out, a fresh sea breeze rippling the women's veils and dresses and softly rustling the palm trees.

They allow Mary and the child to mount a she-ass who up to now had carried water. Donkey looks on in pain. Unable to carry his lady and undeserving, too, he limps on weakly. Joseph puts the packsaddles and blankets on him, gives him a slap and a good fistful of salt, and lets him to take a long drink of water. How good Joseph is!

The sun is dropping behind the first desert dunes. This is Egypt now. They pass settlements, encounter other caravans, and in the evening spy the first houses among palms, fig trees, and mulberries. Here live shepherds, peasants, and fishermen, gentle people who come out to see the travelers pass by. They pitch camp between some walls, ruins from a distant past. Mary dismounts and Joseph returns the she-ass. They light the fire. There is refreshment in rest. At last they are in the land of Egypt. The caravan people come to say good-bye. Before dawn they will set off in another direction.

The little girl comes close with her milk mug.

"Lady, are you tired?" She kisses the baby for the last time. He looks at her wide awake, as if grateful for everything she has done for his mother. Mary kisses her and gives her a little silver coin.

"God be with you, little one."

8

$\mathcal{A}$ Diamond in the Sand

THE NEXT DAY, AGAIN ALONE, THEY BEGIN their journey under the sun. At mid-morning they rest at the foot of palm trees beside an old well, near the tents of nomad shepherds camping nearby. Their children run about, and their cattle cluster together in the shade. The shepherds look at them curiously and sell them milk and dates. In early afternoon, they resume the journey.

At nightfall they arrive at another oasis with several wells, abundant vegetation, and people camping in multi-colored tents. Several curious children come out to see them. Joseph asks the parents' permission to spend the night close by, watchful above all for the safety of Mary and the child. He unloads the donkey, gives him as much to drink as he wants and a handful of barley, which he chews slowly, so exhausted is he. They are allowed to stay near the common fire, expressing their thanks by signs, and there they heat their simple food, which they eat thankful to God and at peace with the world.

At night the breeze carries the smell of the sea not far away. Through the palm trees the stars twinkle in a clear sky. Mary holds the child close to her upon the donkey's packsaddle and gives him her breast. "How tiny! The Son of God!" And with only the warmth of her lap and Joseph's vigilance to defend him. Donkey also seems to be watching him, eyes heavy with sleepiness and fatigue.

Mary falls asleep with the child wrapped in her mantle. Joseph places more bark on the fire and covers her feet. *How weary she seems, but how serene her face seen by the light of the flame! And how calmly the child sleeps.* "Lord, You wanted this journey; guide us where we must go, lead our steps as You led those of our fathers when You brought them out of this land." And Joseph also falls asleep, vanquished by fatigue.

Mary wakes when it is still dark to give nourishment to the baby. Faint red light behind the dunes to the east announces that the sun soon will rise. She places the child, still sleeping, on Joseph's lap. His hair is rumpled and his beard shaggy. She puts on water to boil and places dough in the pan to make some fried patties with a little lard and salt. Joseph wakes up and picks up Jesus, kisses him, and places him upon his chest, while watching the rising sun now above the horizon.

What a great mystery! God Himself, for whom this sun is no more than a grain of sand in this desert, lies here on my chest—so small and defenseless. But Herod has not been able to overcome Him! Now we are in this strange land . . . for how long?

"Joseph, come and eat something."

Joseph gets up, hands the baby to Mary, and goes to give the burro something to drink from the old leather bucket.

"Donkey, we are here at last. This land isn't bad if someone works and keeps to himself. So now you know what to do."

Donkey looks at him as though he wishes to understand. Joseph sits down next to Mary and takes a long drink of water, still fresh from the night dew but salty. He eats in silence while watching the child who laughs and does patty-cakes. He asks God that this be the end of the incessant trudging under the sun. They say good-bye to the people who took them in and begin the journey on foot, slowly but without pause. Donkey follows, head low, ears down, steps unsure. He is hungry and would like to eat some moist grass. He follows Mary, the child, and Joseph, and this brings him comfort. This is his life—to follow the way pointed out to him, rain or shine, cold or hot, hungry or filled. Near the three of them, the monotonous steps of each day take on meaning and so do his work and weariness.

They meet some humble peasants and ask them in the universal language of signs and smiles about the next settlement. The people point them toward the west, at the same time observing them curiously. Covered in desert dust, they are like any other strangers, and yet there is something in their speech, their looks, their humble yet dignified bearing that raises an unanswered question. Finally they come to a settlement flanking the caravan route. Dogs bark from the houses; curious children draw near. Joseph asks directions and is pointed to some dwellings at the far end of the village. Arriving, they knock and wait, hopeful hearts lifted up to God.

"Lord, your son is in his new land, the one You directed us to—an enemy in other times, now vanquished and defeated like Israel. May these good people receive us." The door opens. Questions, then a smile, an embrace, and "Come in"—into the welcoming shade.

After a week, they leave for Heliopolis, a small, ancient city with a sizable Israelite colony. Acquaintances of Joseph offer lodging in their small, humble abode, which the infant sanctifies with his presence and Mary beautifies by cleaning it. They are an elderly couple whose children long since left to become traveling merchants who only occasionally visit their old parents. They are simple working folk, who have adopted their neighbors' language and customs while keeping the faith of their fathers.

In a few days Joseph finds work as a mason. The weather is hot and humid. He spends hours under a harsh sun placing adobe bricks in long, symmetric rows traced by twine and plumb lines. As he works, his mind flies to God, to Mary, to the child. He learns some words of this strange tongue, amid smiles and grateful gestures to his companions. Around his head he ties a thick cotton band embroidered with ducks, that Mary gave him to catch the sweat. Mary usually comes at midday to bring him lunch in a small wicker basket hanging from the arm in which she holds the baby. The child brightens at seeing Joseph, covered in limestone but full of love. They eat with Joseph's fellow work-ers, sitting on the grass in the shade of a wall.

"Oh, Mary, lovely among all creatures, more beautiful than the moon and the sun yet humble and unrecognized, only a woman of your times in a foreign land!"

Mary also works. She looks after the child, does the domes-tic chores, and helps the owner bake bread to be sold outside the house. She is up before dawn to knead dough fermented by yeast. Taking small chunks of it, she skillfully shapes them to be placed in the oven now ready to receive them. The landlord uses a large fire shovel to place the baking bread on polished bricks.

The first sunlight breaks over the horizon, and the first batch of freshly baked bread is ready to be placed in baskets. When the baby wakes, Joseph picks him up and goes in search of Mary. She joyfully gives them warm buns.

◆ ◆ ◆

The seasons go by. Mary and Joseph's life, like an overflowing fountain, carves its continuous course in work and at home. The child grows, strong and healthy, and learns to say his first words, mingling the languages.

On Saturdays they go early to the nearby synagogue. Then, after putting the house in order, they often spend a day in the country beside the beautiful, clean river that in the delta con-verges with the great Nile. Donkey bucks in happiness while Joseph bridles him to carry Mary and the child, who is already enjoying the outing. When they arrive, they choose a secluded, shady spot with grass or soft sand, and there the baby learns to take his first steps, wobbling between Joseph's and Mary's arms. They enjoy watching the flight of the herons, the fishermen taking silvery fish from their nets, the river vessels that pass by slowly, propelled by the rowers' poles. Ducks flutter nearby, beating their wings, scattering the water, and repeatedly sub-merging their multicolored heads.

Mary sets out food on a clean cotton tablecloth, the simple fare of the poor on a weekend outing, seasoned with love and a dash of art. Acquaintances and their children sometimes join them at lunch, happy of heart and thanking God for the gifts received from His hands.

One of these countrymen, a fellow worker with Joseph, has taught him to fish. With their clothing tucked up, they plunge into a small marsh nearby, and there dig with their hands in the mud to find bait that they keep in receptacles hung around their neck. Sometimes their faces get splashed with mud, and the child and Mary laugh at seeing them get even dirtier as they try to clean it off.

Next they look for a good place to fish. Having found one, they bait their hooks and throw them skillfully to midstream. Soon there is a tug, the fishes bite but get away. Again the weighted lines are tossed, until some unwary fish gets hooked. Everyone is thrilled, children shout, and Mary admires its size.

Before sunset, they gather in prayer. The child has fallen asleep in Mary's arms, worn out from the excitement of the day. Returning, they often stop by the humble home of a countryman and work companion of Joseph's, sick with a fever that won't go away. An older man who has found work and refuge in this country, he lives poorly, accompanied only by a lad whom he has taken in. Now his deep-set eyes shine with happiness at the sight of this family that has come to see him. "Thank you, thank you for coming; I don't deserve it," he says repeatedly.

Mary straightens the room, picks up the dishes, and prepares food. Her presence, beauty, and smile bring hope within those poor walls. Joseph cleans the sick man, arranges his blankets, and tends him with efficiency and affection.

They eat with the sick man, converse with him, pray together until night falls. Then they return home, the child still sleeping in Mary's arms, the proud fishing rod held high by Joseph.

◆ ◆ ◆

Egypt is a peaceful country, at the same time rich and poor, with no great extremes, no great hates or grand saints. Days, weeks, and months go by in the monotony of daily work done face-to-face with God and face-to-face with man for this small family come from far away.

Mary gets to know an Egyptian neighbor, a young woman of unkempt beauty with several small children. Married to a local merchant, she is overwhelmed by caring for the children and disenchanted with life because of marital conflict.

The couple's house has an ample interior courtyard shaded by tall walls and an aged bougainvillea that dyes the white-washed walls bright red.

Mary befriended the young mother as she was out rounding up her little ones from the street with frequent shouts and threats. Mary helped her, carrying Jesus in her arms, who enjoyed watching the youngsters play. The children looked at her curiously, one of the girls welcoming her by running to her and saying, "Miriam, Miriam!"

Acquaintance blossomed into friendship. This good young woman had let herself be mastered by bad temper, due to the burden and boredom of having to raise her large and ungovernable brood by herself. They communicated by signs. Some afternoons they went to the inner courtyard and, the children having been fed and calmed down, the young woman would teach the language to Mary, who learned rapidly. Her companion stared at Mary admiringly and, gradually, with affection. They used papyrus rolls bearing the first part of Holy Scripture in Egyptian which the husband had brought back as an object of curiosity from one of his trips. In a few months Mary was speaking the language correctly. Jesus prattled his first words in both tongues.

The woman related her life story, her disappointments, her troubles and joys. Mary told a little of hers, so very different. The woman couldn't understand why they had abandoned their land to come here, crossing the desert with the little child. How difficult for humans to understand the divine plan!

As Mary spoke, her friend observed her closely and watched the lovely child taking unsteady steps. No matter what Mary said, the other was mystified at the enchantment of this friend who was changing her life by her example, discreet words, and simplicity. But so it was: every day she was in better temper, the house was neater, and she was better dressed. She rose at dawn, had more time for household chores, treated the servants more kindly, and even found time to paint ceramics, an art she had learned from a famous master when she was young. The husband began coming home earlier, and his trips were not as frequent. He met Mary and the child and now and then visited Joseph's humble abode.

One day Mary spoke to her friend about God. The woman, not much of a believer, held a superstitious faith in various divinities and went to a temple with her husband occasionally, but her beliefs played no real role in her life. Mary told her about a unique infinite creator of everything that exists—the star-studded sky and of this world we live in and the bird singing close by. She told her of an all-powerful God who loves us with the love of a Father and wants us to respond to His love in action and in truth.

And she spoke about good and evil, about the soul and eternal life, about prayer and the value of sacrifice.

"Mary, will you teach me to pray? I believe in your God."

And this is how that woman became pious and good. She freed a slave whom she was accustomed to treating badly and forgave all her relatives with whom she was on bad terms. No longer vain and superficial, she became respectable and charitable, a source of joy to her own and an example to acquaintances.

At the beginning of his second spring, Jesus can toddle around the house. He waits for Joseph's arrival and, hurrying to him when he comes, lets himself be lifted, kissed, and cuddled; they laugh together. The family has adjusted to this welcoming land, speaking its tongue and living its customs without forgetting their own traditions.

One day God speaks again to Joseph in a dream, clearly and precisely: Herod has died; they can return to their land. Joseph cannot get back to sleep the rest of the night. He thinks of the journey. The child has grown too big to be carried and the donkey couldn't stand it. What if there is another desert storm? Better to go by boat to the coast of Palestine as many traders do.

At dawn, after washing up, he finds Mary bustling about.

"Mary, the angel of God, the same angel that spoke to me in Bethlehem, has revealed to me this night that King Herod, he who wished to kill the baby, has died. We can go back to the land of Israel."

Mary holds her breath. She is filled with joy, yet a little sorry to leave this new home, their friends, neighbors, and acquaintances, and this hospitable land. Looking at the child, her hand on a cradle, she says: "Jesus, my son, you will again be without a bed, as in Bethlehem, and traveling defenseless, except for my arms. We return to the land where you were born, to our people."

Joseph listens and says: "I thought about making the journey by boat. What do you think of that, Mary? That way we will avoid that cruel desert and shorten the trip."

They begin to dispose of their few possessions. Joseph sells his tools, gives away his fishing tackle; Mary, her kitchen gear and the furniture they have acquired. They say good-bye to their sick friend and to their acquaintances. Mary bids farewell to her neighbor friend, who weeps inconsolably. She has learned to love Mary with all her young and noble heart. She gives Mary a blue linen mantle embroidered in silver. Mary, having little, gives her a ringlet of the child's hair. "Take this. It is most valuable to me and will be valuable to you. Keep it close. May God be always with you and yours. Good-bye."

"Mary, I will always pray to your God and my God. May He accompany you."

Everything is clean and in order on the day they leave. His employers give Joseph a big basket full of food. Joseph shoulders the burden, prepares the donkey with the old packsaddle, and over its haunches places the full knapsacks. They set out. As they pass the house of the friend, saying good-bye through the veil that covers up to the eyes, the voices of children are heard:

"Miriam, Miriam, come back . . ."

❖ ❖ ❖

It takes only half a day's journey on a flat road among houses and orchards to reach the port. At the pier several small vessels are loading and unloading; Mary remains on the bank of the river with the child, looking at the waters that stretch to the horizon under a blue, cloud-crossed sky. Sea gulls fly about screeching. There are smells of tar and dried fish. Children are playing nearby. People are coming and going, getting on and off the ships.

Joseph goes to the captain of a sloop to arrange their passage. They are three—the child doesn't count—since the donkey comes with them. The captain objects to the animal. They argue over the price. Joseph doesn't want to leave the beast behind, and he persists. He can see the donkey on the shore beside Mary. Donkey seems to look sad, as if sensing he may be left behind; he stands with hooves planted in the sand, mane blown by the wind. Joseph insists the animal will be needed to carry his wife with the child in arms after they land. He raises his offer a little. At last the captain agrees upon observing Mary, who carefully holds the child while he tosses handfuls of sand in the air.

Donkey doesn't want to walk up the gangplank. He stops, retreats, lowers his ears. Joseph speaks to him, energetically yanks him, and gives him a couple of whacks on the rump. Finally, he goes up, almost dragging Joseph. Mary laughs and the child laughs because she is laughing and because he is excited about the journey, the swaying boats, and the children who are running about aimlessly.

They board the boat and get settled with the sun high in the sky. A man from Joseph's workshop arrives at the last minute, bringing fresh fruit. Joseph takes it and embraces him. The man stands on the shore with others who wave as they leave. The sail goes up and the wind fills it. Timbers creak as the vessel moves to midstream. Mary, seated, waves and raises the toddler's little hand. "Say good-bye, my son, to these people and this land that welcomed us."

The river is wide, and the far shore can hardly be seen. Geese fly by, honking loudly. Fishermen look on while slowly drawing in their nets. Flying fish flutter above the water like threads of silver. Mary and Joseph look joyfully on this new scene and praise God in prayer: "Lord, how beautiful and admirable is the work of Your hands. How much beauty You have created for us and for Your son!"

A lazy crocodile slides through the bank's mud toward the water. The passengers, safe on board, point at it and laugh.

Reaching the estuary, where the tides ruses in from the sea, the little boat sways as it cuts through the waves. The wind tosses shreds of foam that wet the travelers. They disembark at the bay's big wharf. Before them lies the sea, blue, immense, with sails silhouetted against the horizon, the odor of saltwater in the air, the constant sound of waves washing the sand.

Here awaits them a big seafaring vessel, a Phoenician name on its prow beneath a rusty anchor. Its sails are furled; its crew is busy on board. Donkey takes wavering steps on land, seasick from the rocking of the boat as it cut across the flow of the tide. Joseph, also somewhat seasick, takes him by the halter and leads him to a trough of water, but he doesn't drink. The beast boards the ship along with other animals.

Making themselves comfortable among some cotton bales, they eat in silence as night falls. The ship's deck lights are lit awaiting the hour of departure. By the light of the moon, passengers settle down on the deck. The sails are unfurled, the ropes are loosed, and the vessel slowly moves away from the wharf, while the lights of fires on shore mingle with the stars in the sky.

The child has fallen asleep. Mary and Joseph seek to make themselves comfortable among the bales and sleep to the rhythm of the ship's soft, rhythmic swaying as the waves break against the bow. Mary's prayer springs forth when she raises her eyes to the dark, star-studded sky.

"We are going back to our motherland, Lord. Great and mysterious are Your ways. Here we have learned many things, we made friendships, the child grew. Jesus blessed this land with his presence, and it welcomed us as pilgrims."

At daybreak, life begins to stir on the boat. A lively boy with dark eyes and a bright smile comes to play with Jesus, who is taking his first steps on the deck under the vigilant watch of his mother. Mary lets him to go to the little boy, who receives him with hand extended while Jesus laughs. The father of the child approaches.

"My name is Alphaeus, and this youngster is my son Levi—or Matthew, as he is also called. I am a merchant. We are going to Caesarea, but my home is in Tiberias. And you?"

"We are going to Israel, our motherland," says Joseph, "to Bethlehem of Judea."

Alphaeus looks at them with interest. "Bethlehem—that is where Herod had all the children killed a couple of years ago."

Mary and Joseph are dumbfounded, horrified. Now they understand the angel's haste, the precipitous journey at night.

"They say Herod will be succeeded by Archelaus as ruler over Judah. May God protect us. Like father, like son."

Joseph is thoughtful. He is beginning to doubt the wisdom of going back to Judea. Alphaeus knows many people and is worldly wise. His conversation is pleasant and picturesque. It captivates the couple, while Jesus plays with Matthew. The trip becomes shorter and more agreeable. Joseph thanks God, for it is good when traveling among strangers to find a knowledgeable friend.

They encounter other vessels with billowing sails that gradually disappear over the horizon. Dolphins jump and play in the ship's wake. Mary lifts the boy to see them, and he claps with his little hands, laughing. His mother shares his delight, while letting her hair blow in the afternoon breeze. "Joseph," says Alphaeus, "the color of your wife's eyes blends with the sky. Never did I see so lovely a mother and child."

Mary prays: "My God and my Lord, this sea and these fishes You have made beautiful so that we may glorify You in contemplating them. And this precious sky, ever changing and ever the same, now blue, now red, with great white furls at the horizon. And there You are, Lord, and here Your Son, between my hands, enjoying Your creatures."

A flock of pelicans goes by, skimming the waves. Matthew points at them.

"It is said that pelicans pierce their breasts with their beaks to feed their young with their own blood when they have nothing to give them to eat."

The sea voyage goes rapidly in good weather and with a good sea. The first mate takes advantage of a southerly wind to steer the vessel to the east. Joseph sleeps under the stars to the rocking of the waves. The angel again speaks to him in a dreams: "Do not go back to Judea."

In the morning, the sailors point to the coasts of Palestine in the distance. This is the land loved by the Lord. As they get closer, mountains and trees can be seen. The ship docks in Gaza. A curious crowd watches. Joseph descends with Alphaeus, and they meet some acquaintances of Alphaeus. Joseph asks who now rules in Judea. "Archelaus is king."

Joseph boards the ship again, and speaks to the captain: They will continue on to Caesarea. He hands over most of the few coins he has left. Poor they left this land, and poor they shall return.

He, Mary, and the boy buy some fresh food, then forage for Donkey. The beast thanks them with a swish of its tail for the generous bundle of grasses Joseph brings him.

They spend the day not far from the vessel. Merchandise is unloaded and new merchandise brought aboard. The stevedores work, the traders talk, people come and go; new passengers arrive and wait at the gangplank. They wait in the shade of an ancient ruined wall, tense, tired, and hot. At times the child cries and then sleeps. Mary prays. Joseph keeps looking at the boat as though afraid it will leave without them.

Allowed on board in the afternoon, they find to their bitter surprise that they have been robbed of all their belongings and food. Nothing is left but the donkey's packsaddle. Mary calms Joseph down. "It was our fault, Joseph; we did not foresee this."

Alphaeus arrives with his son and servants. After listening to Mary, he lends them some blankets. "As long as I have, you shall not want for anything."

A refreshing breeze rises. A blind man comes on board carrying a long toothless saw on which with stringed bow he plays melodies that remind them of the old songs of their land. The child laughs; they become quiet. Mary gives the blind man a coin, and having taken it, he remains before her.

"Lady, may I touch your boy?" He places his hand on Jesus's head while his lips move in prayer.

At high tide, they unfurl the sail, and the vessel starts to move. Mary concentrates on her prayer.

"Lord, You gave us these small things, memories of this country, and You permitted that these things our work had earned be taken away. Blessed be Your will. One must not become attached to anything. Everything passes; everything is made and unmade in a moment. Our hearts are in You, Lord."

◆ ◆ ◆

Caesarea is a big port, where ships and merchandise constantly come and go. They arrive on a gray morning with a light breeze barely pushing the vessel over quiet waters to the dock. Alphaeus's servants and pack animals are waiting, and the animals are loaded. They say good-bye to the captain and go ashore.

Mary rides on the donkey. Joseph, on foot, shoulders their few remaining possessions. They quickly take a last glance at the ship resting quietly on waters that gleam in the setting sun; a flock of screaming gulls passes overhead. Crossing the noisy city, they take the road that leads toward the mountains of Galilee.

Donkey is happy; no more standing on those constantly moving planks—now his hooves make tracks in the sands of his land. Once again he lends his back to Mary and the child, now grown heavier, and proceeds sure-footedly ahead. How lucky he is! To serve and work for Jesus, Mary, and Joseph, and for them to suffer weariness, hunger, thirst, solitude, fatigue, and injured hooves. None of that matters as long as he can hear that soft and energetic voice that calls to him while simultaneously pats him on the neck.

"Donkey, hurry. Soon we will be home!"

It is autumn. The days are growing shorter, the leaves turn-ing yellow and the grass brown, as the last summer flowers wither. Swift birds fly close to the ground with cries to guide their young. The storks are flying high toward the south. Mary points them out to the child who, laughing and clapping, looks everywhere except upward. She watches him with happy eyes and rejoices in her heart. Soon she will be able to show him to her own people. What has become of her parents? How have they fared? Only through an occasional passing merchant has she been able to communicate with them, learning that they were well and had set aside their initial anguish to accept God's will in the confidence of Mary's return some day.

Alphaeus, riding a strong she-ass, doesn't stop talking about events of the past and ones to come in the future, about har-vests, trade, the simple people who work the fields through which they pass and curiously greet them. Mounted on a mule, Matthew believes himself a true horseman. A servant's hands provide protection against a fall, while the boy grows impatient to be home.

On the second day they reach Nain. Alphaeus hands over Jesus, whom he has been carrying in his arms, and they say good-bye. He kisses the child and Mary's hand and gives Joseph a warm embrace.

The mountains of Nazareth can be seen in the distance. Mary's heart beats faster, and the donkey quickens his pace, sensing his stable ahead. Joseph lengthens his stride.

"Look, Jesus. Your land, the land that God your Father chose for our people, the land that has given so many saints and prophets. How many souls await you there! They have waited centuries for you, my son, my Jesus."

They reach the town's first houses, unchanged in their absence. Children who look familiar watch. Some women turn their heads and stare curiously. They climb the steep hill so familiar to Mary, and in late afternoon reach the house of Joachim and Ana. Red flowers at the entrance blow in the breeze.

Neighbors peek from the doors of their houses. Doves flutter near the porch where they were eating. It is silent. Joseph helps Mary dismount. She gives him the child and knocks on the door with the palm of her hand.

Since they first learned of the flight to Egypt, Ana and Joachim have accepted the will of God with supernatural vision and human anxiety. Life has continued at the same pace: work, prayer, silence, happiness. The news from Egypt lifted their hearts and lessened their sadness at the absence. With Herod's death, their hope for a speedy return had been reborn.

A dog barks from within. The door is a long time opening. Joseph sees his house in back, the fig tree with its withered leaves, the myrtle. The child in his arms observes everything with open eyes. Mary arranges her veil and her clothing. The door opens. Ana stares at the newcomers, torn between doubt and wonder.

"Mother, it's us. We are back from Egypt!"

Ana emits a cry, then hugs and kisses her daughter profusely.

"Daughter of my heart, praised be God who has brought you home safe and sound! My little one, my little Jesus, my child and my God. Come, let me hold you. Joachim, Joachim, it's they, they have come!"

Joachim comes quickly but awkwardly, cautious because of his failing sight. He cries out excitedly: "Mary, daughter of mine, blessed be God. Thank You for returning her to her home in a goodly hour! And this is Jesus, my Lord. How beautiful he is! Come, let me see him close. Bless you, Joseph, may God be always with you!"

Servants and field hands, neighbors, friends, relatives all arrive. They bring lamps, for the sun has gone down behind the mountains. Stars twinkle in those heavens that touch the earth in Nazareth.

9

Human Love, Divine Love

Months go by. Joseph has transferred his workshop to the small house where they live next to Joachim's. His clients follow him because he is a good worker—trustworthy, truthful, "honest as the day is long." Through the small courtyard half-covered by a grape vine, he can see the interior of his home, where Mary bustles about doing chores and Jesus plays.

Joseph works a lot and works well. The cuts are straight, the wood well brushed, angles exact, pieces of furniture well assembled. In the cold of winter and heat of summer, he must often go out to finish jobs, coming back soaked and muddy if it is raining, or covered in dust in times of drought, hands red if the job was fixing a roof or white with limestone if it was repairing walls.

Furniture, beams, staves, doors, and windows come from his carpentry shop, spreading his fame as a good carpenter through Nazareth. Sometimes, while Mary is sewing or spinning, Jesus watches him from the courtyard, hands grasping a railing Joseph has placed at the doorway to keep him from coming in and hurting himself with the tools. Seeing him, Joseph puts aside brush or saw and, lifting him in his arms, carries him inside. Jesus enjoys the sight of those bright tools, the polished boards, the shavings everywhere, and the characteristic smell of recently cut wood.

"Look, son, this is my workplace; here I earn our daily bread with the sweat of my brow—as our Father God directed in

Paradise—along with the callouses on my hands. Here I offer my work up to God and sanctify myself. Here I carry out the greater part of the task for which I was born. All of us have much to do in life. I begin here, without rebellion or complaints. With joy."

The child looks on, laughs, says a few words in his baby talk. When he reaches for a sharp chisel, Joseph takes him back to his mother who, with her sewing on her lap, has watched the scene from a distance.

In early evening Mary takes her son with her to feed the chickens. Jesus runs after them hoping to catch them, frightening the doves and disturbing an old cockerel who looks at him haughtily.

His mother gives him a handful of grains which he throws to the fowls, turning then to look at her, well pleased with what he has done.

Jesus learns to put together his first syllables in simple and familiar phrases. He speaks like any child in this land and begins by naming the father, "Abba," and mother, "Immi." Mary feels profound joy at hearing herself so named. It is her son and her God calling her Immi. She repeats words to him, corrects him, repeats them again, until he learns how to name people, things, animals. She applauds and he smiles.

Joseph also takes him in his arms and carries him to the orchard or the corral where Donkey is kept. Donkey happily lets himself be given a few soft slaps by the child. Joseph shows him the animals, naming them. How precious is the joy he feels in teaching Jesus, Son of the living God, as he learns like any other child in his father's arms!

Mary feeds him spoonful by spoonful while Jesus laughs, plays, tosses pieces of bread to Doggie, and prattles. Mary also laughs, insists, and offers prizes or punishments like any mother feeding her young.

The child sleeps serenely in his cradle. Just after midday the song of Ana's little bird is heard. Mary is working not far away at embroidery, and Joseph is in the workshop, muscles tensed over the rough tools that cleave the wood. Mary goes to the fountain. Joseph passes by the child as he sleeps under the vines. Drying the sweat from his forehead, Joseph stands there watching him, something he never tires of doing even though the child is so near day after day. Sitting down next to the cradle, he prays. Mary returns and, sitting down beside him, joins him in prayer.

"Mary, how happy I am, so close to you both. Blessed be God who placed you in my care! May He give me strength to protect you."

They live in that dignified poverty that comes with few possessions and honest work. Mary keeps everything clean, tidy, and neat. She uses what God gives her, from a stray needle to fallen fruit, making the most of everything. This and the knack of making the ordinary lovely are skills she learned from Ana. And so she puts quinces in the linen chest so that when they ripen, they will spread their aroma through the house every time the chest is opened.

At night, in the first light of the oil lamps, Joseph washes up before going to see his parents.

"Are you tired, Joseph?"

"Surely, Mary, you must be. You have this house looking like a palace."

"It's more than just a palace, Joseph. It is the dwelling of the great King. And so small. See how he is always laughing. He likes everything, and it makes him happy, just as he makes us."

"You say well, Mary."

In the parents' house, Ana prepares her grandchild's bath in the old tub of cured wood held together by strong iron bands.

"Mary, let me bathe him."

"Mother, you always ask me that."

"Yes, daughter, it is the best time of the day for me."

The fire is lit; lamps give a flickering light. Jesus likes the water very much. He plays, splashes, enjoying himself while chattering in his baby talk. Ana scrubs him with great care, pours water over his hair once and again. The child laughs, and throws water at Doggie who frisks away. Finally Ana puts Jesus on a clean towel on her knees and dries him, feeling his heart beat under her arms and looking upon him ceaselessly.

"How beautiful he is! His eyes are so bright!" His little plump hands caress her face. "He reminds me of Mary as a baby!"

Sitting next to the fire, Joachim observes the scene.

"Thanks, Lord, for this child, this son of Yours whom You sent to these Your people, to this house of mine. How lively he is! He looks like the other children of this land, yet he is not the same. How does my humble home deserve such happiness?"

"Give him to me, Ana, while you straighten up."

Ana gives him the child, already dry, dressed, and combed, his hair still wet. Joachim places him on his lap, embracing him.

"My little one, my Savior here in my arms. My child, let me look at you well. I want to etch your face in my mind."

Mary comes for him to take him home and give him supper.

"Good night, Mother. Good night, Father. Say good-bye to Grandma and Grandpa, son." She holds up his hand to wave.

"God be with you, Mary."

◆ ◆ ◆

Like the lights and shadows that pass across the sundial that Joachim embedded in the wall, chiseling its numbers with an awl, the years go by quickly. The child grows, walks by himself, talks. The grandparents grow old. When Joachim returns from sowing, he takes him from Mary's arms. But soon Jesus is running about by himself beside Doggie and lets himself be picked up.

"Grandpa Joachim, what have you brought me?"

Joachim searches his pockets with a doubtful look and almost always brings out some fruit or a toy affectionately whittled the night before. Then he holds him while Jesus enjoys his presents. When they arrive at Ana's, she as usual is sewing. She expertly peels the fruit and gives it back to him to eat then and there.

"Mother, you're spoiling Jesus. He can eat that fruit by himself."

"Daughter, how happy it makes me to be able to do so! Wait until my sight fails me and my hands shake. Then I will stop spoiling him."

The fire crackles in the hearth. Joseph arrives, still drying his hands on the white towel that Mary brought him. Jesus runs to him and he lifts the child, asking for a bite of his fruit. Jesus happily gives it to him.

"That was a big bite!"

Everyone laughs. Mary laughs with the loveliest sparkle in her eyes, she is so happy with this child. And with Joseph and her aging parents so close, she doesn't mind the work or the scarcity or the heat and cold, the dust in the summer and the mud in winter. Neither does she mind the monotonous life of this small town hidden away in the mountains of Galilee. It is better this way—they can be more at peace, far from the ambitions of the mighty and the deceptions of intriguers.

Doggie happily gnaws the pit from Jesus's piece of fruit.

When the weather is good Mary likes to take Jesus with her while she does the wash in the stream that winds through the valley of Nazareth. This is where Mary played as a child when she came from Jerusalem in the summer. Jesus relishes being in the water. He loves to chase after fish, look at dragonflies resting on the rocks, toss thin pieces of bark that become little ships that sail with the current and, capsizing, are shipwrecked in the reeds, and wade after them in his bare feet while getting wetter and wetter. Bending to scrub, Mary watches smiling from a distance. Occasionally, if lucky, Jesus catches small frogs and brings them home. He releases them in the orchard fountain, and in the afternoon they come hopping into the house.

In summer they like to go to higher ground that Joachim, with Joseph's help, has planted in the spring. Hopefully they will watch their crop ripen at summer's end. Here crickets sing. Joseph teaches Jesus how to catch the shy black insects, which Jesus puts in small cages of dry woven rushes. At home he gives them lettuce and happily applauds when their singing alternates with the chirping of Ana's bird.

There are days of labor when all the grownups work together on that dry, impoverished land while the little ones pretend to help. At noon, they come together in the shade where there is abundant water. Mary and Ana arrange the simple fare, brought here in Donkey's packsaddle. While they eat, Donkey swishes his tail and munches on sprouts.

Jesus runs about, picking small flowers that he brings eagerly to his mother. Her hair gathered in a shawl and holding a hoe, she receives the little bouquets with a smile. He also brings her little white stones and sometimes an egg fallen from a nest that he regards as a treasure.

Jesus talks and talks. His voice resembles his mother's, with a mountain accent. Those near him fall silent briefly and contemplate him until they resume work.

Mary of Cleophas accompanies them whenever she can. James plays happily with Jesus. His mother holds a small one by the hand and another at her breast. Cheerful Mary hasn't lost her sense of humor, despite her difficulties and pregnancies. She is a strong woman who knows God will not abandon her. Cleophas, more blessed with offspring than with business, hasn't lost his sense of humor either. Some days he stays over and joins the group in the evening. He dreams of his enterprises and still admires Joseph.

Sometimes on the high ground, rain catches them by surprise. The sky darkens, the wind blows leaves and weeds, and they huddle under a leafy tree as the thunder draws nearer, lightning flashes in the clouds, and lightning bolts terrify them. Sheltered under blankets, Mary cuddles Jesus. They feel impotent.

"Abba, where does the lightning come from?"

"They are manifestations of God's power, son."

Donkey, head lowered, stands nearby, the flashes of lightning reflecting on his soaking hide.

The storm passes. There is the smell of wet earth. Small birds fly low, crying to one another as they snatch up winged ants coming out of the ground. The torrent rushes between its banks, carrying with it rocks that make a dull crashing sound as they collide.

A timid sun dyes the sunset red, announcing that it's time to go home. A fallen nestling flaps about, chased by children until it lies trembling in Jesus's hands. He watches it and pets its head. Joseph promises to make it a cage, and Mary tucks it carefully in a little basket.

They go back. Joachim rides the donkey, with little James on its rump. Joseph bears Jesus on his shoulders, glad to carry so sweet a burden. Mary wraps the shoulders of them both with her mantle.

◆ ◆ ◆

Now Jesus begins to learn to read the Holy Scriptures. Joachim would have wished to be his teacher, but his sight is failing. So after Joseph goes to work, Mary brings out the timeworn scrolls and patiently begins to teach him. She is amazed at how rapidly Jesus learns; young as he is, he retains all the words.

"Son, tonight you have to recite this song to Grandpa. You'll see how pleased he'll be."

"Immi, would you like me to recite the names from Grandfather back to Adam?"

While talking to her son, who sits on a raised straw mat, elbows on knees, while his hands play with her embroidery, she fingers his hair, and finds it full of straw.

"Look at your hair, son. Wherever have you been?"

"I went into the straw loft after some chickens to see if they had laid eggs."

"Don't go up there anymore, son. That ladder is not safe."

"Yes, Immi."

Mary keeps teaching words to her son, taken from the texts of Holy Scripture, until, like any other child, he tires and loses concentration.

"Go and play, son. That's enough for today."

Jesus, now near the age of reason, rides Donkey alone. He likes to make the beast run with a cheerful trot, jump, and even gallop. There is a yard with thin grass next to some of Joachim's plants, and there he can ride to his heart's content and have races with James, who follows behind mounted on Cleophas's old mule.

Jesus grows stronger. He is agile and has light brown hair and large eyes like his mother's. He sits firmly against the wind on his mount, dodging obstacles and guiding the faithful donkey with his heels. Mary is vigilant from afar while she works in the fields with the rest.

One afternoon, the children chase a rabbit, and he runs away hippety-hop. They pick up sticks and run after it. Running and shouting, they go far from the little yard. When it seems they are within reach of the rabbit, it dodges them and escapes. The boys fall down among shrubs that leave them scratched. They spy the rabbit hiding under some boulders. They are sweaty, out of breath, lost. Then a dog barks furiously. He stands beside a shepherd observing from a hillock next to his sheep.

"Be quiet, Goliath."

The children approach the white-bearded man. He has bright deep-set eyes, worn clothing, and weather-beaten skin.

"Where art thou from?"

"From Joachim's pasture grounds."

"Art thou brothers?"

"No, cousins. My name is Jesus, and this is James."

"Jesus, Jesus—and your parents?"

"Joseph and Mary."

The shepherd crouches down and, taking Jesus's hands, looks at him intently.

"In the temple, years ago, my brother Simeon held a baby called Jesus in his arms . . ."

He rises.

"I will lead you to your fields."

He pulls out a small turtledove from his sheepskin and gives it to Jesus.

"Take it. When you look at it, remember to pray to God for this old shepherd."

"Thank you." After looking at it, he gives it to James.

"No, it is for you. I already have one."

After walking a while, they see Mary and Joachim, who signal to them from afar.

"Immi!" shouts Jesus. He begins to run, followed by James.

"We were chasing the rabbit!"

"Don't go so far away again. Just look at you!"

With a soft handkerchief, Mary cleans the scratches made by the thorns.

"Mother, a shepherd gave me a turtledove. Look."

Mary smiles and presses his tousled head to her bosom.

Before Jesus has reached the age of discernment, his parents take him to Jerusalem for the first time. It is early spring. He rides on Donkey. The sights and sounds are all new to him. He observes everything, laughs, asks questions, and helps—as much as his strength allows—in everything.

Mary rides on another mount, remembering the sights of this busy road. Joseph prefers to walk, happy at taking care of this child and mother whom he respects and loves more every day.

"Abba, is this the place at the river where you were assaulted?"

"No, son, the Jordan is farther east. It is much more beautiful and wider. In summer this year we will go to Tiberias, and you will get to know it."

When they reach Jerusalem, Jesus falls silent, staring at its old crumbling walls and its enormous structures that grow white under the afternoon sun.

"Immi, are we going to the temple today?"

"No, son, early tomorrow."

Jesus prays with Mary in the Atrium of the Women. They gaze toward the sacred place. Their souls rise in dialogue with God; they are not distracted by the people coming and going. Joseph comes up to take Jesus to the Atrium of the Jews, where only Jewish men of his people can enter. Jesus prays next to Joseph, too. They are not in a hurry. They have not come to the temple just to perform a duty but to pray to their Father God.

After a few days, having fulfilled the prescriptions of the Law, they go to Ein Karem to visit Elizabeth before returning to their land. It is a warm spring day; the fields are still green, and the wagons make ruts in the wet clay. John opens the door to them. He has unruly black hair and dreamy eyes. Mary kisses and hugs him tenderly: How much she loves him! Jesus hardly knows him, but greets him with a kiss. They look at each other in silence for a while until Elizabeth arrives and, with joyful exclamations, hugs Mary and bends to take Jesus in her arms.

"Jesus, Jesus! Let me look at you. You came here in the womb of your mother before you were born. Oh, blessed God, flesh of our flesh you are! How tall! He looks so much like you, Mary!"

Zachariah arrives presently, leaning on a light walking stick.

"Ana's grandson! The Emmanuel. Come close, son, that I may have a good look at you. 'Your face I wish to see, Lord.' Strong hands, eyes like his mother's. Praised be the Lord! What does your voice sound like, son? Speak something close to me, for I no longer hear very well."

"Grandfather Joachim sends you his kind regards."

"Thank you, son."

They all walk into the shelter of the big old house, still cozy as ever, whose well-preserved plinths make it look ancient now. Field hands and servants arrive to greet them and serve them.

Presently, John takes Jesus to the stables to show him where, a few days ago, a thin and slender goat was born. Zechariah shows Joseph the house. Mary and Elizabeth have so much to tell each other! Mary opens her soul to her dearly beloved cousin and friend. She tells her of her desire to comply in everything with the will of God, of the most chaste love of Joseph, of her humble and hidden life filled with household tasks, and above all of her total devotion to Jesus.

In these crowded days Jesus and John get to know each other, making friends and coming to love each other like brothers. As souls chosen by God, Mary and Elizabeth share a profound joy in what God has entrusted to them.

"What will become of these sons, Mary? The world will not love them."

"God is with them, Elizabeth. Remember the psalm, 'I have chosen thee ever since the establishment of the earth; you are my son.'"

One afternoon common relatives of theirs arrive, tired and covered with dust. They speak of rumors of an uprising in Galilee. They have seen soldiers on the march and travelers who bring alarming news about deaths and fires in the villages.

Sooner than foreseen, the visitors prepare to leave. Zechariah embraces Jesus for a long time, tears rolling from his tired eyes.

"My son, I have a premonition that I will not see you again on this earth. God will reunite us in heaven."

They travel quickly yet serenely. Nothing will be gained by tiring the mounts uselessly. Jesus continues to enjoy the small events of the trip: a crested bird that appears suddenly on the road, a peasant selling freshly picked fruit. Mounted soldiers pass by. Mary hides her face behind her veil, and they leave the road. The riders glance at them with indifference. Beyond Sichem more soldiers come from the opposite direction. With them carts with equipment and tattered prisoners in bonds, faces marked by defeat and suffering. Jesus is now on Mary's mount. He looks at them intently.

"Immi, where are they taking them?"

They arrive at Nazareth in the evening. A platoon guarding the outskirts stops them.

"We live here. I work as a carpenter. We come from Jerusalem."

"Leave the mule. The ass does not interest us."

Mary and Jesus dismount. Joseph takes her belongings and helps her get up on the donkey. He leads Jesus with his other hand. Wearily, they begin the climb to their house. The streets are dark. No one is out. There is fear in the air.

A pale Ana with sunken eyes opens the door. Doggie barks.

"At last, children, praised be God. Come in, come in."

"What's happening, mother?"

"It began in Sepphoris. A man called Judas stirred up the town. He gathered followers and took to violence. He seized arms and mounts. The group grew until the troops came and began to pursue them. They have killed many and made prisoners. The others have been scattered. Now they are hunting for them and their sympathizers."

"Joseph, do you know any of them?"

"Some I know."

"You are in danger. It would be best if you hid."

"I can't leave them by themselves."

"Mary and her little ones hid in the cave. Cleophas is in hiding."

"I will go with Jesus to the cave, Joseph. You hide."

Jesus listens to the conversation with heavy eyes. Finally he falls asleep and his mother takes him to lie down. They eat some of what Ana has prepared. Joachim dozes by the fire.

"Mary, I wouldn't want to leave you."

"Nothing will happen to us, Joseph. Things will settle down in a few days. I'll prepare warm clothing and everything you need."

Ana watches Joseph's pale, fatigued face.

"What was the journey like?"

"Fine, Ana. With Jesus and Mary, one can go anywhere—it's like heaven on earth. But you aren't leaving?"

"No, we are just a pair of unimportant old people."

Joseph takes his packsaddle, which is bursting at the seams, gives a kiss to Jesus, who sleeps serenely, says good-bye to Ana with a hug, kisses Mary lightly on the hair, and walks into the night.

"God be with you, Joseph."

"May He be with you."

The cave is uphill, hidden among brambles and rocks in a dry ravine. Several women and children are hidden there. After unloading Donkey, Mary settles herself among the others, next to Mary of Cleophas and her children.

Quiet at first, Jesus finds James and they go out to explore. Mary is silent, praying: "Lord, we are in Your hands; deliver us from evil. Protect Joseph and my old parents; be merciful to these people and these poor souls who are being persecuted."

Hours pass. The silence is unbroken. Night falls, and it grows cold, but they are afraid to light a fire. Mary of Cleophas's small daughter cries. Mary picks her up and makes her comfortable in her lap.

"My *talitha* [little one], don't cry."

She calms down. They sleep; angels stand guard; stars shine outside.

Dawn finds them cold and anxious. The children go out to play and collect firewood. Discomfort and fatigue have left their mark on these people. They talk very little and doze. Mary of Cleophas smiles at the tenderness with which Mary freshens and dresses her little daughter whom she begins to call Talitha.

Another night, another uncertain dawn. Hours go by. At noon, there are voices and the sound of horses' hoofs. Soldiers are approaching. The people press together in the cave.

The soldiers enter, and the officers dismount. There is a brusque search. Doggie barks furiously. A spear thrust pierces his heart. He whimpers and is still. Nobody moves.

"Is any man hidden here?"

"None, only women and children."

They survey the group haughtily. Mary remembers a similar scene twenty years ago in the house in Jerusalem. It's the same story—oppressed people defenseless before their oppressors.

"Cornelius, do you want us to torture one so that they'll tell us what they know?"

The Roman looks at them arrogantly. He notices Jesus, who meets his gaze.

"Leave them; let's go."

The soldiers carry away blankets and food, smash water containers, and leave.

Silence. James's little sister cries. Mary rocks her in her arms and calms her.

"Talitha, it's over now; don't cry."

"They have gone!"

Ears pricked, Donkey looks on from a distance, as though wanting to understand. Jesus and James drag Doggie to a cleft in the rocks and cover him with stones.

"Brave Doggie. Why did they kill you?"

A night of anguish, fires in the distance.

"Oh, Lord, what has become of Joseph? Have they found him? Protect him. You Who are almighty, we only want to serve You, allow us time to love You. Jesus needs it; he is small. Lord, look at these times and my elderly parents; I soon will be without them."

In the afternoon two young women sent by Ana arrive: Now they can go back.

"Is everybody all right?"

"The only took the fodder and the mules. There is nothing left to eat."

"We'll manage. Let's leave."

Days go by, but Joseph does not return. Anguish and intense prayer continues. Everybody prays. A serious Jesus spends much time crouching next to the hearth where Joachim sits. Between their comings and goings, the women pray; prayer brings them together in God.

On the midnight of a rainy day, there is knocking at the door. Ana, keeping vigil, approaches it with an oil lamp in her hand.

"It is I, Joseph."

He enters. His beard is shaggy, his hair disheveled. He is pale, thin, and wet to the bone.

"Is everybody all right?"

"Yes, son, everybody, thank God. Come, get close to the fire."

Mary comes running, hugs Joseph, and cannot contain a sob against his chest. Jesus is lifted from his bed and hugged with feeling.

"Cleophas has also come back. He is at home."

The uprising has ended in a bloodbath. Judas and some followers were left on crosses on the outskirts of Sepphoris. When their bodies were removed, the rains washed away any memory, any trace of them in the land of their birth.

◆ ◆ ◆

The synagogue school gives the children vacation to help with the harvest. Jesus comes home joyfully. He will go out to the fields with his family and his cousins.

But as they have done yearly, before gathering the crops they go to Tiberias to spend some days in the home of their always hospitable kind host and good friend Alphaeus. He is thankful for the days this humble family spends under his roof.

The wind carries the smell of the Sea of Galilee to the small river town. Jesus, riding Donkey, wants to go faster, and soon he sees those sweet waters with blue mountains in the distance. The breeze whips up little waves that break on the shore. Here is a boat, sail unfurled to the wind, fishermen are shouldering their net. Seagulls fly by screeching.

Although he is a little older than Jesus, Matthew loves and respects him and seems naturally ready to follow his lead. Matthew's mother admires Mary, and tells her this is where they come for a rest and to eat fish that they never taste back in the highlands. Their room has a window overlooking the lake from which they can see the setting sun reflected in its waters and at early dawn the fishermen setting out hopefully in their boats.

Jesus and Matthew ready their little canoe to go out and fish until the south wind begins to make waves. Jesus rows for a while and Matthew casts the line; then it is Jesus who tosses the bait and happily waits for a bite. The sun beats down, and the breeze makes the water splash against the oars. The blue sky is dotted with small white clouds.

God looks upon the world and in it his Son, for whom He created all things and made them beautiful like these blue waters and this sandy shore.

At last a fish lands at the bottom of the boat, where it flops about for a few moments. Then another and another. There is nothing after that except the frequent bites that make the bait disappear. They pull up on a beach, tie up the boat, and throw themselves happily into the water. They swim, splash about, come out, then dive in again.

Other boys approach, fishermen from distant shores, who show them a pair of large fish recently caught with the casting net. These are exchanged for bread, fruit, and a few coins that foresighted Matthew brought along. Then they all swim together, happier than ever.

"We are from Bethsaida. I'm Andrew, and this is my brother, Simon. We came with our parents to fish."

"I'm Matthew from Tiberias, and this is Jesus of Nazareth."

They dry themselves on the beach in the sun and decide to eat a large roasted fish. They share food and friendship. Then it is late, and they say good-bye.

"Good-bye. We'll see one another again."

Mary and Matthew's mother are waiting on the beach. Joseph is fishing nearby. The waves brake gently over the sand; the wind bends some reeds close to the shore. The small canoe with the two boys comes in sight. Mary's heart beats faster when Jesus comes ashore and runs to her.

"Immi, we have a big fish and three small ones."

"I'll fix them for supper."

Joseph approaches with a broken rod and tackle.

"I wasn't lucky." He smiles at Jesus. Mary smiles at them both. Soon they return to Nazareth.

❖ ❖ ❖

Jesus attends the synagogue school regularly. Mary sees him off daily together with James, who drops by for him. There is always a kiss at the door and another one from Ana, who always manages to be at her door when they pass her house.

The men labor; the land yields its fruit. Children are born to fill the emptiness left by those who die. Joseph's workshop is popular, and he is kept busy from dawn to dusk.

Mary hums to herself while she works. Talitha, the daughter of Mary of Cleophas, stays with her while the mother is again in labor. Always smiling, with eyes as black as her hair, she laughs when she talks and talks with a laugh. There is no school here for her to attend, so Mary teaches her things that she learned in school.

Jesus is twelve. He is growing stronger, and his voice is changing. This year they will again go to Jerusalem for the Passover. The fears of sedition are gone.

The caravan is numerous, the journey slow but pleasant. Mary rides Donkey, who is happy and contented. They no longer have the mules. Oh, precious burden, how lucky he is! Joseph, with Jesus at his side, walks at a good pace; James and his younger brother Simon happily join them. Mary enjoys seeing them walk nearby, laughing. At the resting places they gather firewood, fetch water, pitch the tents, and listen to Joseph's reproach.

"Woman, I've got almost nothing to do nowadays!"

Going up to Jerusalem, the groups come together. The many pilgrims sing ritual psalms, Joseph in his deep voice, Mary in the beautiful voice that she still possesses, Jesus with a juvenile voice full of fervor.

Mark's wife awaits them, brimming with joy along with her husband, with little John Mark in his arms. The lights are lit, the water in the fonts prepared.

"Welcome to this your home."

"God bless you for your hospitality."

Jerusalem is full of foreigners. The Roman garrison is watching for the least sign of trouble. Merchants, eager for sales, prepare their wares. The little blind boy, now a man, is begging for alms in the same place.

Jesus enters the temple with Joseph, while Mary remains in the Women's Atrium. They pray, spiritually absorbed while pilgrims come and go around them. Reunited at the exit, they find a group of doctors of the Law in discussion with foreigners who ask them questions.

Other families and friends come for the Passover Feast until the great hall is full. Before they eat the lamb, Jesus must ask the head of the family the meaning of these rites. Mark answers, ending with these words: ". . . by these prodigies we must praise and glorify Him who has changed our tears to joy, our darkness into light, and only to Him must we raise halleluiah." Everyone joins in the hymn of praise, "Hallel."

Mary observes her son across the table. He wears new robes, and his face is illumined by the light of the oil lamps. Her heart overflows in an act of thanksgiving.

The seven days pass, and they are ready to return home. Mark and his wife bid farewell to the pilgrims and fill their packsaddles with food. The women cover their heads with their veils. They leave.

Soon after leaving Jerusalem, they join the caravan of fellow Nazarenes. There are reunions, shouts of joy, happiness and contentment all around. Their caravan falls in place behind others in a long line heading northward. Mary, on the little donkey, loses sight of Jesus. She supposes him to be with Joseph toward the rear. They travel for hours, along winding roads among olive trees. At midday they halt at the stopping place of El Bireth. Joseph comes up by himself.

"Where is Jesus?"

Joseph goes up and down the caravan. No sign of him.

Mary remains with James and Donkey at the side of the road.

"Oh, Donkey, where is Jesus? We have lost him."

Donkey looks at her with moist eyes, trying to understand. He has already lost her once, on the journey to Egypt. How much he has regretted his cowardice! This time he will not leave. He stands firm, faithful, at Mary's side.

Joseph hurriedly inspects the other caravans, all the way up to the lead caravan. Hours pass. Mary, longing to see the face of her son, sees the last caravans go by. James offers her something to eat.

"Thank you, son, not now."

It is growing dark. A dusty, perspiring Joseph arrives. Nothing. They go back to Jerusalem.

"Dear God, what could have happened to my son? Lord, how endless this road has become. Has the king, son of the one who wanted to kill him, discovered him? Lord, You placed him in our trust. He is Yours. Give him back to us."

"Don't cry, Mary. We'll find him. Remember, he has a mission."

Back to the house in Jerusalem, where lights still shine in the windows. Hope rises, then fades when they find he is not there. They rest until the next day.

Before sunrise they go to watch at the gate of the caravans. One after another they go by, noisy and carefree. They go to the temple. The last pilgrims are leaving. They scour the squares and streets; they ask relatives. Night falls.

"Mary, you must rest; tomorrow we will find him."

"Yes, Joseph, you also need to rest."

Once again, early, they watch at the gate of the caravans; these are the last to leave. They return again to the temple. At the exit of the Atrium of the Men, a group of doctors of the Law is listening attentively: Jesus is standing in their midst. He questions them and answers when they are silent. These teachers are astonished. Taking advantage of a pause, Joseph draws near.

"Son, we are looking for you."

Jesus says good-bye to those erudite men and leaves with Joseph to rejoin his mother, who hugs him and covers him with kisses. They are welcomed joyfully at Mark's home. Sunset gives way to a serene evening with stars twinkling in the sky.

Back in Nazareth, Jesus no longer attends the synagogue school but works in Joseph's workshop. Now his life as a carpenter begins, and in summer that of a farmer. With Joachim and Joseph he works the land, its stony and unrewarding soil worn out by erosion and lack of water. Here he learns about good seed and weeds, thistles and thorns, sowing and reaping, a day's work and day workers, rain and drought.

He begins to do some carpenter's work on his own. He makes a low chair for Joachim and weaves its wicker by himself.

"Grandfather, it's so you can sit close to the hearth."

Joachim is failing. A lifetime of hard work has taken its toll, as has the saintly death of Zechariah. Not only is his eyesight going—his heartbeat is becoming erratic. Every day when the weather is good, Jesus spends time with him in the orchard. Joachim dozes, prays; he never complains. One day he cannot get up. Ana stays at his side. The agony begins. Several days pass. He dies serenely, the scrolls of Sacred Scripture beside him. Jesus keeps vigil beside the body.

Ana is strong. She hardly cries, though inwardly she feels the loss intently. So many years together! Her hair is completely white now. She asks Joseph and Mary to move into her home. The little house will be used exclusively for the workshop.

❖ ❖ ❖

Donkey has a new stable, all his, and he begins to daydream. He wants to be like those swift horses that run across the fields with their manes flying. He doesn't want to carry dirty firewood or heavy sacks of wheat anymore. He dreams that Joachim saddles him up and sends him to a town in the valley. He trots, he gallops and . . . suddenly he can no longer run. His hoofs are like lead; he stops, head down and breathless. He goes back to his stable and accepts it when once again he is set to carrying firewood.

Months go by, the rains come, and the land softens. Joseph rents strong oxen that pull the plow and break the hard clods. Again Donkey dreams: This is his job: to plow, prepare the land for sowing. Joseph harnesses him to a small plow. Before him lie ruts in which puddles reflect the sun. He begins cutting a furrow when the plow encounters a root. Donkey pulls, digs in his hoofs, stretches his neck to the utmost, wears himself out while the plow stays as if nailed to the ground. Exhausted, he goes home and humbly lets himself be loaded with sacks of rye to be taken to market.

More months go by. Donkey soon forgets the past. One morning he sees the mules depart, their harnesses lustrous, laden with provisions for the workers up in the mountain. Once again he dreams. He's going to be like those strong beasts of burden that mount steep paths to the heights. Joseph puts a new packsaddle on him with two tightly fitting baskets at the sides, places a balanced load on him, and sets him at the head of the train so he can set the pace. Donkey starts well and moves briskly on the flat land, but as the ground rises he starts to feel faint; he can no longer go on. The mules overtake him and keep on going. Donkey is alone, crestfallen. This is not for him. He goes to the stable's farthest corner. A smiling Joseph gives him a pat and a lump of sugar. "Donkey, your job is to be a burro and work wherever you are placed."

Donkey wakes up and sees Mary closing a window and smiling at him.

He stops dreaming and works hard. He helps Jesus and Joseph, carrying wood, taking newly finished furniture, bringing the firewood Mary collects, water from the fountain, wheat to make good bread.

One day Donkey comes up from the valley with two long logs whose trailing ends make furrows in the earth and slither over stones. Joseph pulls him by the reins while Jesus keeps the logs in line. Near the house he stops; his heart fails him, and he has trouble breathing. Jesus releases him from the lumber, and Joseph, tugging on the reins, manages to get him nearer to the door. He arrives almost lifeless. Mary comes out and looks at him with concern.

"Donkey, Donkey, what is wrong?" She caresses his forehead and neck. "My faithful Donkey!"

Jesus brings him water, but he doesn't drink. Joseph removes the packsaddle. Donkey's eyes go up into his head, those moist eyes that have so often looked upon Jesus, Mary, and Joseph. He falls to the ground. Joachim acquired him fifteen years ago in Jerusalem, soon after he was born. With his head on the ground and his eyes closed, the white star on his forehead looks brighter than ever before.

◆ ◆ ◆

"Before God, no occupation is in itself great or small. Everything gains the value of the Love with which it is done" (*Furrow* 487).

Jesus works full time with Joseph at the workshop. Gone are those happy days at the school, the outings with his mother to the river, and the carefree games. He begins to mature in the sight of God, his parents, and the people, drawing a man's strength from his work as a carpenter.

Mary brings her loom, her sewing chair, and, on cold days, the brazier onto the far side of the courtyard. From there she can see her son, working from dawn to dusk under Joseph's direction.

These are happy years, with no lack of sorrows and joys, roses and thorns, to temper love and full acceptance of the will of God. They labor well, doing flawless work fit to offer to

God. At midday, a frugal lunch, like that of the people of that land; Joseph asks God the Father to bless the nourishment they receive from His hands. Mary goes back and forth from the table to the fire, and Joseph lays the plates.

The winter cold enters mercilessly through the small slits in the roof. Shavings and chips of wood burn in the braziers, spreading the smell of resin through the house. When firewood grows scarce for the brazier, Mary keeps close while working; she goes to the workshop and they make room for her near the narrow opening covered with lambskin that has been smeared with lard and tightly stretched. The light is meager and the space very limited, but now happy they are there! Joseph works serenely and by his side Jesus, growing taller and filling out before her eyes.

When it snows or rains or the wind blows constantly, they don't go out. That keeps the heat in longer. And their hearts are joined in mutual love that fills Mary in a continuous act of thanksgiving to God.

Some days relatives or friends come to share a meal. Joseph invites them in after offering them jars of water to wash themselves; Mary always has a clean towel ready. Jesus, smiling, listens to them talk. Mary asks about people, prays for their troubles. Joseph presides.

In the early afternoon Joseph and Jesus are accustomed to take an outing, seated on the she-ass, or to do the various jobs of artisans in a small town—thankless and often poorly paid work done in cramped quarters or in danger of falling, like replacing tiles on a wet and slippery roof, cold wind buffeting face and hands, repairing a broken door, or rebuilding a mud wall that has crumbled in the winter weather.

In the evening they come home tired, covered in dust and limestone, their hands battered and numb. Mary waits in the light of a lamp, her face flushed from its nearness, hair drawn up, hands clean, a penetrating look in her eyes, and a ready smile on her lips. While waiting, she has prayed:

"Oh, Jesus, son of God, admirable son, man of labor, so modest: were it known who you are, those boards you lovingly worked upon would be kissed, and those biting winds would cease hurting your face and hands!"

Hearing his steps at the door, she rises quickly and kisses Jesus even though his face is white with limestone. Then she waits for them to change their work clothes for other homely but clean and warm apparel. They draw near the hearth, rest, talk quietly, heart to heart, communicating more by gestures, looks, and tenderness than by words.

Wrapped in her thick mantle, Ana keeps the embers going on the hearth and the food ready; she cannot help kissing everybody whenever she can just as she always has. Often she takes Jesus by the hands.

"How cold they feel! Son, don't keep on growing—you are already taller than your grandfather; you are like a cedar of Lebanon."

Ana is growing old, but she stays active. Her gaze is intense, her memory lucid, and she is always busy, always attentive to details, unmindful of herself; she remembers everybody—those present, those absent, and those who have already passed on.

They have supper and gather around the fire. Some relative or friend is always visiting. This is a family that attracts, not so much for its riches as for the inner light it radiates. There, visitors know, nobody speaks ill of anybody else, for in this home God is loved.

Beside the hearth, Mary sews the last stitches of the day. She meditates.

Jesus—what will become of him? How much longer will he be with them? And Joseph? He looks tired. It's that illness he picked up on the flight to the mountains. It comes back in winter! Why doesn't he complain? He only smiles and works, but she sees in his face the weariness of sleepless nights.

When the first stars are in the firmament, they retire to their quarters, where the love of God is warmer than the embers still glowing in the hearth.

Ana's little bird proclaims spring with its happy song. So do the cooing of the turtledoves in the myrtle, the first rose on the bush Mary brought from Jerusalem, the little turtle that appears in the orchard, and the arrival from Ein Karem of John. When he was little he used to come with Elizabeth, but in these last years he has come alone or with a houseboy. Mary loves John so much! He is like a second son, so similar to Jesus yet also so different, with curly black hair, a thick beard even in youth, thoughtful in expression and few in words, a little shorter than Jesus. He is a restless and austere dreamer.

"Aunt, my mother sends you all her love with me. She is well, but she is sad because she couldn't come."

He makes himself comfortable in the room next to Jesus's. Sleeping on the floor and eating whatever comes along doesn't bother him. He spends months in Nazareth studying the Scriptures that Joachim had collected during his life. He is affectionate at times, gruff at others, spending hours in the orchard immersed in prayer, heedless of cold and heat. Now and then he goes to the workshop and stays there for a long time watching Jesus. He tries to help him, but soon declares himself too awkward and gives up.

They worship and pray together, alternating the psalms. Mary, standing nearby unobserved, is touched by what they say about God. On feast days, agile and quick, they climb a high mountain behind Nazareth that has thick forests and a splendid view. They come back tired and contented, their faces reddened by the wind at the summit. Mary welcomes them joyfully. Food is steaming on the hearth.

As the first rains soften the earth for the winter, they work in the fields. John works zealously, listening with pleasure when Jesus speaks to him of sowing and reaping, weeds and crops and birds—the lore of the fields taught him by Joachim. As time passes, the love of brothers grows between them.

The old pear tree in the courtyard of Joachim's house sheds the red leaves of autumn. In winter it is a bare trunk with jutting branches. Come spring, it sprouts dark green new leaves and white flowers that attract the bees. The small, hard fruit soon appears. It grows slowly and ripens in summer.

Ana looks forward to the day they are to cut the golden pears that greedy wasps have already begun to enjoy. Jesus expertly climbs the tree, armed with a long cane, while Mary and John wait below holding a large blanket into which Jesus's soft taps cause the fruit to fall. Ana carefully picks them out while throwing reproachful glances at John for those which he clumsily lets drop. Mary laughs. In the end, Grandma gives half a pear to each.

"So they will last and you won't tire of them," she says, cutting them with an expert eye.

Summer over and the crops harvested, Jesus and John go to Mount Tabor, whose summit is visible from Nazareth. In their knapsacks Mary packs food and overnight blankets sewn up to resemble sacks. On the day of departure, she awakens them at dawn, her hand on her heart, a smile on her face.

"God go with you. Come back early. Good-bye."

Mount Tabor is lonely, rocky, and desolate, hot in the day, cold at night. A shepherd greets them from the slopes and looks on curiously. The distant blue of the Mediterranean can be seen on a clear day from its pinnacle, the heights of Mount Carmel. Farther south are the rocky crests of Samaria, which slope down to the spacious planes of the Valley of Esdraelon, site of ancient battles and stained by the blood of a people's young men. Toward the east lies the distant Valley of Jordan, even farther south is the sea of Tiberias, rimmed by the Mountains of Bashan.

They pitch a tent held up by old boughs and branches to protect them from the sun during the day and the dew at night. They pray, talk, and contemplate their surroundings. They spend the night gazing at the immensity of the stars, suggesting the infinity of God to whom they give their last thought before they sleep. And so pass another day and another night. At daybreak, having prayed together and watched the sunrise, they set out on the journey home. On the way they pass through the vineyard of some relatives, affable and hospitable people, who give them something to drink and abundant grapes.

Mary is waiting with her sewing in her lap. The sun goes down, and often she hears sounds that she imagines are footsteps. At last they arrive. There is stubble on their chins, their clothes are rumpled, and their happiness at being home is clear on their faces. They smell of thyme and bring her a big bouquet. Jesus gives her some clusters of grapes. John says he meant to bring her some too. Mary puts them in a bowl and is the last to taste them. Joseph praises them and gives thanks. Ana is waiting next to the hearth.

"John, you are just like your father. Can't you see that your cloak is inside out?"

Everybody laughs. Joseph begins the evening readings while Mary sets the table.

❖ ❖ ❖

One year John didn't come. A hot summer was followed by chilly autumn winds at harvest time. The epidemic began in the lower hamlets. Joseph's parents, siblings, and relatives fell ill. In a short time someone was sick in every home in Nazareth, breathing with difficulty and getting sicker and sicker. Silence and terror grip the little town. The streets are empty, and there is weeping indoors.

Ana and Joseph take to their beds. Mary and Jesus look after them. Ordinary work is suspended, life is upended; time passes slowly. After the cold winds comes suffocating heat. The sick grow worse, suffer, weaken. Mary of Cleophas arrives terrified: her husband is very ill, as well as her youngest child and her parents. Jesus goes with her to help. Mary is alone. Joseph is in his room, pale, with a growth of beard. He breathes with increasing difficulty, but he smiles when she comes near. Mary spends much time sitting at his side, drying the sweat, holding his burning hands, watching his haggard face. She prays.

"Lord, don't take him away yet. We need him. He has lived only to serve You and love You, and he has loved us."

Standing firm in her faith, she doesn't cry.

The day goes by slowly. Jesus returns in the evening, pale and fatigued. Mary is alarmed. She helps him lie down close to Joseph, then spends the night awake, keeping vigil over them and over her mother who is suffering next door, attended by an old maidservant: What a terrible night! Mary, stalwart, trusts in God.

The day breaks hazy with heat. Joseph hardly breathes. Jesus sleeps restlessly. He wakes up with the light.

"Oh, son, ask God your Father to save him for us!"

"I will ask him, Mother. You pray, too. I will keep helping in the town."

At mid-morning Ana worsens. Her serene countenance reflects the peace in her soul. She smiles when she hears her yellow bird chirping. She opens her eyes in the evening.

"Is Jesus well?"

And she dies in the arms of Mary. Her soul flies up to rejoin Joachim. They lived together, and together they shall be forever and ever in Glory. Mary lays her out alone, wiping her silent tears with the edge of her sleeve.

Back home, Mary notices that Joseph is breathing more easily. His eyes are peacefully closed. Jesus sleeps. Worried and exhausted, she lies down for a couple of hours. Mary of Cleophas, accompanied by her daughter Talitha, wakes her up. Both are crying disconsolately. Cleophas has died, praying to God and begging forgiveness. He would have wanted to see Joseph.

"Oh, Miriam, what will become of me and my nine children? How am I going to live without him? My God, My God!"

"Mary, whatever I have I will share with you. Your children will be like my children, like Jesus's brothers and sisters. Give Talitha to me now."

Mary embraces her and cries gently in the arms of Miriam, finding there the strength to go home and remain firm at this bitter time.

At mid-afternoon, pious men who risk their lives and make no concession to their weariness take Ana to be buried. Faces veiled, Mary and the little one accompany the cortege through deserted streets. Nazareth is a different place—even the birds don't sing. They return home.

"Aunt Mary, why does this happen? Doesn't God love us?"

"Yes, daughter, God loves us a lot. These things happen so that we may be purified. One day you will understand it. Your father will go to heaven, and from there he will see you."

Jesus comes back. When he hears of Ana's death, tears fall from his reddened eyes. In silence he embraces his mother. Joseph gets better. Sip by sip, he drinks broth given him by Mary, then placidly sleeps.

Another day dawns. A light, refreshing breeze blows. Linnets sing in the myrtle.

"Joseph, your parents have died and Cleophas, and his youngest. The epidemic is passing."

A tear rolls down Joseph's weather-beaten face. This is the first time Mary has seen him cry.

"May God receive him in His bosom."

The town goes back to its old life. Tears give way to work. Some wounds will never heal, some laughter never heard again. Only the love linking those who stayed and those who departed remains—that and the hope of seeing one another again, thanks to firm faith in the promises of God.

Joseph and Jesus take up the workshop tools again. Mary looks after Ana's little bird, which never sings. Mary's hair has threads of silver now.

❖ ❖ ❖

The years go by in Nazareth. Monotony binds together everyday happenings that seem to have no importance yet do when weighed in the scale of eternity.

There is hubbub and happiness in the house at Nazareth. Cleophas's children often go there: They work, play, laugh, and eat everything they can lay their hands on. Talitha helps Mary whenever she can; She is pious and obliging. Judas and Joseph, serious and formal, toil in the workshop. James goes to the fields and follows the rules of good farming that Joachim taught. Mary of Cleophas continues to wear mourning clothes but hasn't lost her smile. With her many children comes the courage possessed in abundance by generous mothers.

Toward the end of one summer, John comes again, tall and thin, with deep-set eyes and an untrimmed beard. Mary receives him with immense affection, but the news he brings about Elizabeth is alarming: she is in very bad health and no longer leaves her room. Mary proposes that she and Jesus go to see her. He agrees.

Joseph prepares the she-ass as so often before. Jesus and John, leather pouches on their shoulders, help Mary mount. She looks youthful and is smiling as on past occasions. Swallows warble; the doves flutter. Overhead is a blue sky and before them a road washed by last night's rains. Joseph says good-bye affectionately. Talitha gives them a basket of fresh turnovers. She cannot help weeping when she says good-bye to Mary.

Jesus and John tease each other, admire the fields, trees, and mountains, greet those they encounter along the way. Mary smiles at them and is happy. The hours seem short to her.

They stop at Jerusalem only to sleep. On the road to Ein Karem next day, they meet a picturesque youth, a chatterbox and extrovert who asks permission to accompany them since he is going the same way. Mary laughs at his tales, his descriptions of things and people. Asked about his home and family, he gives vague, superficial answers. Good and evil are mingled in this youth, products of the misfortunes that have befallen him since he was a child. He says his name is Dismas.

As night falls he asks to sleep near them. He offers to fetch water, spilling a good part of it, and collects firewood. When it is time to sleep, he bundles up in a blanket they lend him, next to a tent and not far from the fire.

Waking next day, they discover that the youth has disappeared, taking with him the blanket, bucket, and food. Jesus and John laugh. Mary is disillusioned.

"Aunt, we'll fast. We'll get home soon. He was more needy than we are."

Jesus picks up the tents. John looks toward the horizons, searching for the youth.

"One day he will be sorry for having robbed poor wayfarers."

They come to a farm where a man and some boys are breaking up the wet earth. Mary offers to buy food from him. Simon the Cyrenean looks at them benevolently, his hand on the hoe.

"Alexander, tell your mother to prepare something to eat for these friends."

The woman invites them to sit on a bench standing under grape vines beside the house. She serves them hot food.

"They took what we had," Mary explains.

The milk Rufo brings them is fresh and still frothy. He does not take the coins offered him.

"Pay us some other time."

"May God reward you and stay with you."

"May He guide your way. Good-bye."

Elizabeth doesn't come out to greet them as she has before. The big old house looks sad—no flowers in the corridors, no shiny floors. Pale and aged, Elizabeth smiles and embraces them from her bed.

"Jesus, my Jesus, how tall you are! John, my son, how much I've missed you. Mary, you look the same; passing time only makes you more beautiful. Thank you for having come."

The days go by swiftly. The patient neither improves nor worsens: she is being slowly consumed like a candle burning down in honor of the Lord. They decide to return. John gives them mules, clothing, and food.

"I don't want anything. When God takes my mother, I will go to a place in the desert, to be alone with God, prepare myself for the revelation of the Messiah, and proclaim it to the people when the time comes. Aunt Mary, I don't know when I will see you again. Jesus—him I will see."

"Good-bye, son, take care of your mother. She stays with me in my heart."

They leave at the steady pace of the mules. The stubble has turned yellow, the trees drop their leaves, and the sky is cloud-covered during the afternoon. The first storks gather in flocks, take flight, and are soon lost to sight.

Mary walks long stretches, holding Jesus's hand. Happy at walking next to him, she finds the journey easy. There will not be many more trips like this one. John will soon leave home. When will Jesus do that? She walks on, tired but smiling. Though silent, they pray on the march.

At sundown they pitch the tent and start a fire. They speak seldom, for speech isn't necessary where love is so intense. They rest while the water boils. "Thank You, Lord, for such a beautiful world, for the setting sun that tints the heavens red. Thank You for being close to my son, Your Son. I do not tire of resting my eyes upon him. I place myself in Your hands, Lord. But please—may he not leave yet."

Near Bethel a youth on a good mount approaches, accompanied by field hands and an extra mule. He greets them. His name is Lazarus, and he is originally from Bethany. He comes from a well-to-do family, farmers of substance, honest and hardworking. A bit older than Jesus, tall and gawky, with a frank gaze and a modest manner, well spoken, he lives with his sisters in a big old house just a stones' throw from the farm. He likes to read Scripture and anything else he can get his hands on and to meditate on what he reads. He possesses the serene calm of a man who nourishes his soul. He has taken the north road with the intention of visiting relatives who live beside the lake.

He is impressed with Jesus and Mary. How admirable Jesus is! His love for him increases by the minute as they talk and he gets to know him. And how beautiful is his mother! Never had he encountered such a woman, neither in Caesarea nor in Jerusalem. Jesus loves his new friend in return. They understand each other, listen to each other with pleasure, and pass beyond earthly matters when commenting on the Scriptures, though at the same time keeping track of their route as good wayfarers should. Seeing God's will at work, Mary does not begrudge Lazarus the time Jesus devotes to him. The young man for his part shows her the deference of good breeding, and she begins to grow fond of him.

After Nain they say good-bye. Lazarus invites them to his home in Bethany; Mary invites him to her humble one in Nazareth. Then they separate. Jesus had found a companion in James, a brother in John; now in Lazarus, he has found a friend.

Meanwhile, for Joseph the days are becoming intolerably long, dull, and gray. He thinks constantly about Jesus and Mary. The more he loves her, the more he respects her. What an admirable woman is his wife, no wonder God chose her! She is unassuming, discreet, hardworking, and always cheerful. Joseph prays, works, glances at the door; in the evening, seated on a bench outdoors, he scans the horizon. He needs Jesus and Mary. Friends and neighbors greet him. Talitha looks after him as though he were her own father. In her Joseph sees Cleophas, the dearly beloved brother now gone. One afternoon, as a falcon circles above calling stridently, he sees far off on the southern road some dots approaching; he shields his tired eyes with his hand.

"Talitha, can you see some mounts on the road?"

"Yes, Uncle Joseph, I hope it's them."

They become lost among the first houses of the town. Moments pass that seem like hours. At last the wayfarers appear over the incline.

"It's them. Blessed be God!"

They get up to receive them.

"Mary, welcome home. Jesus, my son—thanks be to God that you have come back. How is Elizabeth?"

Once again the family is united under the same small roof in Nazareth. They resume their ordinary, monotonous labors with the little pains and joys that sanctify each day's work.

News of Elizabeth's holy death and John's departure to the desert, where people go to listen to him, soon reaches them.

Lazarus frequently visits Nazareth, and there makes himself loved by young and old. His pleasant conversation and love for all captivate the family. Whenever they go to Jerusalem, Jesus and Mary—Joseph, too, if he can make the trip—stop at his house in Bethany and there visit him and his sisters.

❖ ❖ ❖

Cleophas's younger children become carpenter's apprentices. Judas is serious, responsible; Joseph is vivacious and witty, helpful and a dreamer, like his father. They are motivated not only by the small daily wage they receive but by their affection for that family. Their sisters also frequent the house. They enjoy singing together, accompanied by instruments, and dancing holding hands at festivities to which Mary and Joseph are invited.

The happiness of poor working people reigns in that home where love and light abound. Talitha becomes a beautiful and pious woman, helpful to everyone without looking for thanks. She announces that she does not wish to be married, but wants only to live and die beside Mary.

The years go by. Joseph's hair turns gray, his energy fails; that old illness takes its toll. Jesus is strong and tall. Now it is he who takes the saw while Joseph grips the wood. Joseph speaks of the past without forgetting the present. When they go to the fields, after a few hours' work he sits in the shade of the tamarind, looking toward the horizon or at Jesus, still wielding the hoe. No longer does he climbs the roofs: he teaches Jesus to place roof tiles expertly while he holds the ladder.

At night he gets as close as possible to the fire in order to read. Or else he watches Mary, sewing in her hands and fresh strands of silver in her beautiful hair, and Jesus, who is busy tidying the tools as Uncle Ben used to do. He prays, "How good You are, My God, who has given me these years. Full of denials and sacrifices, along with joys and sufferings, but next to them!" Jesus's melodious voice reminds him of Grandfather Joachim, but his eyes are those of Mary; they seem to have infinity in them.

At harvest time this autumn, working with Jesus and the young men, Joseph becomes exhausted. The fine dust of the threshing floor makes him cough and breathe with difficulty. In the work-shop he keeps working doggedly, although Mary urges him to rest.

"I soon will rest in heaven, Mary."

The first rains come, and with them damp winds. Joseph sickens. He can no longer get up. He jokes that he would like to exchange his lungs for a new packsaddle. He worsens as the fever rises. Mary watches over him, imposing silence on the nieces and nephews, allowing relatives and good friends to come in for a minute to greet the patient. She prepares medicines, attends to everything. Lazarus arrives, dusty and agitated. Jesus thanks him for coming. He is a trusted friend who lends a hand, which in these circumstances they are doubly grateful for.

Joseph dreams. He reviews his life. The day he saw Mary at the fountain! His beloved Cleophas, Bethlehem, the desert jour-ney to Egypt, Jesus as an infant, Jesus as a youth, Jesus as the man at his side.

Mary is watchful. Relatives from farther away arrive. Joseph is well loved, a man of faith, a man of work, a holy man. Days go by; Joseph's heart, made for love, does not want to stop beating. His body is consumed by the fever, his voice fades along with his gaze. At the spring moon, he is going.

"Jesus, son, stay by me. Slowly recite some psalms to me so I may hear you."

Lazarus alternates the verses. Nieces and nephews and rela-tives observe from a distance. There are sobs from the women.

Mary, close by, prays with them.

"Lord, each of us has a time to live and a time to die. Joseph is ending his journey. He has loved You, Lord, as few do, and he has served You well, always smiling, always gentle toward me and loving with Jesus. What a grand husband is Joseph!"

Some roses, the season's first to bloom, stand in the big vase in the simple bedroom. Atop a large chest beside the bed lie Joachim's Scripture scrolls. There is fresh linen on the bed. Hanging next to the shepherd's staff Joseph brought from Bashan are some tools, and next to them is a small window through which he watches the sunset for the last time.

His breathing becomes labored. Mary wipes the sweat from his forehead and gives him something to drink that fills the room with the odor of balsam. Joseph breathes more easily, opens his eyes, and takes Jesus's hand.

"My son, my life is at its end. I return to God from whom I came. In Him lies my hope. I have done that for which I was born—cared for you and your mother. I have tried to do it as well as I could, at least when it came to love. How much I have loved! I have worked constantly, and in return I have had your mother's care and your presence to repay me for my fatigue. May God be with you. Look after your mother as I have done."

Joseph closes his eyes. Jesus holds his hand. Joseph turns his head and dies peacefully. A soft sob escapes from Mary, who bends over him.

"Oh, Joseph, in heaven I shall again be with you! You are already with God."

Eyes blurred by tears, Jesus gently places Joseph's hands crossed over his heart. Joseph seems to be sleeping, so serene is his expression. The relatives and friends join in shedding heartfelt tears. Through the window come the calls of birds heralding the dawn, though a few stars still shine intensely in the sky.

10

Roadless Horizon

A thousand graces diffusing
He passed through the groves in haste,
And merely regarding them
As He passed,
Clothed them with His beauty.

—St. John of the Cross

THE YEARS AFTER JOSEPH'S DEATH are not sad ones for Mary, because for those who believe, death is merely a change of dwelling, a time of waiting for reunion that soon ends. Besides, Mary loves and is loved by all those around her, and she has Jesus close by.

In good weather, sitting in the small courtyard in the scanty shade of the vine, she can watch him in the workshop. During the long winters, she sits in a corner of the workshop where she can't be seen by those who enter, observing the workers.

Jesus is now a man. His beard is trimmed, his speech grave, his gaze clear and searching. He has affable dealings with everybody and does responsible work, just as Joseph did. Mary loves him more every day, not certain where her love for God begins and her love as a mother ends.

Talitha has become a woman: gracious and helpful, pious and always solicitous toward Mary, whom she loves with all the might of her young heart; hers is a soul made for love through service—forgetful of self, first to rise in the morning and last to go to sleep. She helps her mother and numerous siblings in every way she can. Together with Mary they weave, sew, and knit by the light of the fire that heats the workshop and fills the house with the smell of burning pine. On the wall is the shepherd's staff given Joseph by a slave, which he took to Egypt. Hanging beside it from its strap is the small horn Cleophas used to call his companions when they were cutting wood in the mountains.

James and Simon join Jesus in plowing Joachim's fields. Mary of Cleophas visits with her younger children as often as she can leave the small business bequeathed her by her husband. The turtledove nests in the myrtle, and when summer arrives it is now Mary who divides the fruit of the old pear tree among the children. These are happy times, not because of material abundance, but because there is love, with honest work and poverty lived in good spirit.

The winter is harsh. Firewood grows scarce, and there is even more reason for Mary to spend time near the workshop brazier. Her hours are filled with love for Jesus and contemplation of God. Now and then, hardly noticed, Talitha goes off to work in the kitchen.

"Talitha, daughter, why didn't you tell me?"

"Aunt Mary, you were so enjoying being close to Jesus!"

Wind and rain lash the little hamlet. Cold filters into the house. At night time they draw even closer to the old kitchen chimney. By its light and that of a few oil lamps, flickering in a draft that sometimes shakes the rafters, Jesus reads the Sacred Scriptures and comments on them to cousins and friends who have come from afar to enjoy the warmth of this home.

Mary also listens with profound inner joy. She is comfortably seated in the wicker chair that had been Joachim's—the one Jesus made for him—her feet well wrapped in a blanket, her sewing in her hands.

In the spring there is news of John. He is in Celim, near the Jordan, and baptizing with its waters. Many come to hear him, repent of their sins, and are baptized. This is hopeful news yet saddening to Mary in its implication: "When will Jesus leave as John did?" One summer afternoon, as Mary is feeding the chickens and the doves, Jesus approaches. Taking her hand, he tosses a handful of barley along with the ones she is scattering for the birds. Quietly he tells her he will leave in a few days to join John at the river. With him will go James and Simon, who will keep her informed. Mary does not let go of his hand while he speaks; she observes his deep gaze and serenely accepts the will of God. She is silent for a while.

"Son, tell me what you want me to prepare for you."

Two days later he announces he will leave the next day. That night Mary hardly sleeps. She spends many hours in prayer. She trusts in God, but as a mother it is hard for her to be separated from her son. "What will this house be like without Jesus? His smile, his look, the sound of his steps, his voice. . . ."

She rises noiselessly while it is still dark. Jesus is already up, wearing sandals and tunic. He greets her in silence with a kiss.

"Remember, son, that Joseph will be married in Cana in two months."

"I will remember, mother."

Smoke from the fire hides the tears that spring to her eyes. A knot tightens in her throat, but she wants to be brave, and she manages it with God's help. Talitha observes in the dim light and doesn't speak, her silence helping more than consoling words. Mary smiles when serving the simple breakfast.

James, Simon, and Mary of Cleophas arrive together with the girls. The tension is broken, much as when the storm breaks when the sun appears. Life goes on. Good-byes, advice. As Jesus leaves, Talitha falls to her knees and kisses his hand. Jesus places his hands over her head shaken by sobs. He kisses Mary. The sun is getting hot. Roosters crow nearby. There is one last hug for Judas and Joseph.

"May God be with you on your road, brothers."

"May He stay with you and protect you."

With firm steps they go up over the hill. Mary stands at the door, her face half-covered by a veil. She watches them draw away. A little daughter of Mary of Cleophas offers her a small basket of peaches.

"Auntie, they are the very first from the tree Joseph planted."

Days go by. After a month, Simon returns, dusty and tired, his skin weather-beaten from the outdoors. His look is thoughtful. He tells of Jesus's baptism in the Jordan, the calling of the first disciples. Now Jesus is praying and fasting in the desert. James and others are there near him.

Jesus returns to Nazareth. He is much thinner, tanned by the sun. His beard is fuller, his eyes deeply set. He is as affectionate and attentive as ever to Mary. Looking into the workshop, he greets Judas and Joseph, and Joseph again invites him to his wedding in Cana the day after tomorrow.

Jesus gathers with his disciples and some neighbors in the orchard, under the old fig tree. Mary and Talitha listen from a distance. This is the first time they have heard him speak in public—divine words, spoken with human simplicity, such as they have never heard before. Mary smiles to herself whenever his listeners don't grasp things that to her are so clear. Before leaving, they ask him to go to the synagogue next day and speak to the people of the town as he has spoken to them. Jesus agrees.

In the afternoon, as so often before, they gather around the fire in the old kitchen. Mary again holds her sewing in her hands, eyes fixed on Jesus. Talitha comes and goes; the cousins and uncles listen with amazement while the little ones watch, half-serious and half-playful. Jesus is at home again. Joseph, Ana, and Joachim are missing, but in their place are disciples, relatives, and friends paying close attention. To Mary, he is the same as ever: her Jesus.

At nightfall, everybody leaves except the disciples, who are to sleep there. They have supper. Mary gladly serves, Jesus gives the blessing. With a distinctive gesture he breaks the bread and hands it about. Mary is beginning to love the men who follow Jesus. She hasn't lost a son but gained many. Saturday dawns, hot and humid and threatening rain. From very early Jesus has been in the orchard by himself. The disciples speak softly while they eat. Joseph says good-bye to everybody, joyful, wearing his best robes.

He sets off for Cana with relatives. Mary tells him: "Tomorrow morning I'll be there with your mother. God be with you."

Mary of Cleophas arrives with her children and helps with the dishes. They leave for the synagogue where Jesus and Mary have gone so often and Joseph was often heard when it came his turn to read and explain the Sacred Scriptures. Now it is filled to overflowing with people waiting to hear Jesus; they can hardly get in and discreetly stand next to the wall in the women's section.

There is murmuring as Jesus enters with his disciples. His white tunic contrasts with his tanned face, darkened by the desert sun. Some exchange words when they see him, others greet him.

Going to the dais, Jesus begins to speak. His deep voice is clear and he is easy to hear. But soon voices are raised to interrupt him; angry people begin shouting. The atmosphere is tense. What is happening? Mary looks on, surprised. Don't they know him? Haven't they seen him many times before? Why this hostility?

They crowd up to him in anger and oblige him to step down from the dais. Mary recognizes the angry ones: some are school companions, some frequent the workshop. *What is happening, Lord?* Jesus remains silent.

Simon, Judas, and James try to defend him so he can depart in peace. They are shoved aside. People are furious. They push Jesus before them toward a precipice not far from the synagogue. The leaders shout. So do some in the crowd.

Mary falls behind those enraged men, who don't let her come near. On reaching the precipice, Jesus slips away. The malcontents return silently, hurrying, indignation still reflected in their faces. Mary comes back with the women, her heart pounding. They don't understand her son! Not even his own people! What will it be like in Jerusalem?

She spends that afternoon alone, praying. Talitha offers her a cup of broth, which she refuses. Where can Jesus be? Did they pursue him? In mid-afternoon James comes to say he is well and tomorrow will go to Joseph's wedding in Cana.

◆ ◆ ◆

Mary of Cleophas and her children arrive at dawn. She is joyful, for her son is marrying a good young woman, neither a beauty nor rich but discreet, pious, and from a good, hardworking family.

They leave; some on foot, some on the donkeys, carrying provisions and gifts, the youngsters in their best outfits with a festive air. Mary wears robes Joseph gave her, which she has not worn since he died. They match the blue mantle she brought from Egypt. Her modest necklace is one that Ana gave her. She is so lovely that the nieces and nephews praise her lavishly.

They reach Cana at mid-morning and soon reach the house, where feasting has been underway since the night before. Joseph greets them, introduces his wife, who timidly kisses Mary, and presents the bride's parents and relatives. The musicians arrive. The merry-making continues in the roughly cobbled courtyard beneath a few colorful awnings. There are tables with food and wine jars. The good cheer of the occasion is that of country folk for whom simply coming together is more enjoyable than savoring delicacies and wine.

In the afternoon, the musicians resume their playing. Friends from even farther away arrive, among them Jesus and his disciples. Hardly able to contain his joy, Joseph introduces him to his young wife, who blushingly thanks him for his presence. Everybody greets these newcomers deferentially. Jesus goes to his mother's table and sits down next to her. Mary smiles joyfully: conversations, music, simple fare—all seem different to her now.

Mary notices Jesus's new disciples, especially one who is much younger. John stays close to Jesus but doesn't stop looking at her with all the affection of his young heart. After spending some time with them, Mary joins the women to help prepare supper. The crowd is large by now. An older man, a relative of the bride, appears nervous and anxious. There is hardly any wine left and nowhere to buy any. He speaks to the bridegroom and the father of the bride, who inspect the empty pitchers for themselves. The men argue, gesticulate. The master of ceremonies has no consolation to offer them. Downcast, they stand aside helplessly.

Mary considers the situation. In the background she sees Jesus and his disciples. His white vestments contrast with the dark robes of his companions. She approaches the table. Jesus smiles at her, the disciples fall silent. Mary sits down and tells Jesus about the wine. Jesus responds firmly, though not without affection. The music for the young people's dancing makes his answer inaudible by those at a distance. She looks at the bride and groom, at the young girls who are singing unaware of the Master.

Mary looks at him, her eyes brimming with kindness, and sees his benevolence; again she makes her request. Jesus takes her by the hand. Turning around, he sees against the wall some stone jars that held the water for purification. Then he tells menservants to fill the jugs to the very top. The disciples watch eagerly as this is hastily done. A few of the other guests watch, too, although most are unaware of what is taking place because of the hubbub. Using a big wooden spoon, the servants taste the good wine that had been water. Amazed, they gape at Jesus. Mary feels like clapping. Mary of Cleophas covers her face with her hands.

They bring a large glass for the master of ceremonies to taste and with pleasure observe his amazement and his haste to show it to the newlyweds and their relatives. Mary smiles a big smile. John watches in admiration and reflects. The wine is poured at all the tables: aged wine, color of toasted honey, which lightens hearts and makes the disciples believe.

At nightfall Jesus rises and says good-bye to the bride and groom. He and his mother exchange looks of affection, and he invites her to come to Capernaum. Mary is filled with joy. John comes close.

"Thank you, lady. God be with you."

"John, take care of him wherever he goes. James, do tell me wherever you are."

Night falls. The air is refreshing. Mary wraps her mantle around her shoulders and retires with the women. The newlyweds and relatives thank her sincerely for what she has done for them. Mary of Cleophas leaves with her, as do the nieces and nephews. The night is clear, with a big moon. The sound of the party diminishes until they enter a nearby house where they are expected.

Next day they travel slowly and pleasantly on the road to Capernaum that curves downhill amid olive trees and green fields of late barley blown by the wind.

The group is numerous. Milling around Jesus besides his disciples are curiosity seekers come to hear him. For Mary, mounted on her old donkey, it is a new experience to be surrounded by so many people, joyful at traveling with Jesus and curious to see her. She is happy that her Jesus is the admired Master, loved by these humble souls who have suffered so much at the hands of rulers and conquerors. Mary of Cleophas is proud at seeing her sons beside Jesus and at the foresight of her daughters, who remembered to bring food for the journey.

At midday they halt under some sycamores that shade a spring. People make themselves comfortable around Jesus. Mary distributes food, helped by her nieces. Jesus watches her with satisfaction.

Seated beside her, he eats in leisurely fashion, gazing on the brilliant waters of the Sea of Galilee. When they finish, he rises. Everybody falls silent; Mary stops cleaning up and sits on the grass to listen. Jesus speaks of penance and conversion, of loving God and all men, of forgiveness. The people, their numbers growing by the minute, listen captivated and nodding. When he finishes, the journey continues along the road through the valley that opens upon the small city.

When Saturday comes, the picturesque synagogue of Capernaum with its handsome stone columns with vistas on the lake is full. Mary finds a good place in the women's section. The attitude toward Jesus is welcoming and respectful, unlike the hostility in Nazareth. Her son speaks for a long time to engrossed listeners. When he finishes, a strange man in the middle of the crowd emits a loud howl—the howl of one possessed—and shouts testimony to him at the top of his lungs. Jesus commands the demon to depart, and the man becomes serene and gives praise to God.

Upon leaving, they are crowded from every side. Peter invites them to his nearby house. Peter's mother-in-law is ill, so she cannot come out to receive them. Mary goes to her room, comforts her, and tells her what has happened. Soon Jesus enters, Peter behind him. Taking her by the hand, he speaks to her and she is cured. Despite Mary's protests, she gets out of bed and serves them.

The day draws to an end. They watch the sunset from the terrace. Its rays are reflected in the lake whose rippling water makes them flash like hammered silver.

Outside the crowd of people who want to see Jesus has grown even larger. They bring him their sick to be cured, eyes imploring, faces etched in suffering. Jesus and the disciples come down from the terrace, and he walks among them, healing as he goes. Mary and the women watch. Her heart overflows with love for those whom her son makes well.

The next morning, while it is still dark, Jesus leaves with his disciples. Already there, waiting since last night in silence, are still more people. Mary wonders when she will see him again. When it is daylight, she leaves to go back to Nazareth.

◆ ◆ ◆

Life is not the same in that dear house. Talitha asks Mary repeatedly about the journey; Joseph, returned from Cana, has told her about Jesus's miracle there. The young husband is at the workshop again, and his young wife serves him.

"Talitha, don't you want to marry, have a husband and a home of your own?"

"No, Auntie, I want to devote myself only to God—to give Him my life and consecrate my virginity to Him. And to serve Jesus and you, Mary, whom I love more every day."

"What will you do if I leave as Jesus left?"

"I will keep on looking after this house until it is destroyed by men or the angels carry it away."

"Talitha, do you have faith in Jesus?"

"Aunt Mary, for a long time—since when Ana was still alive—I have known he is the Son of God."

"Yet his very neighbors wanted to kill him a short time ago."

"God forbid!"

The household work resumes: weaving—now a seamless tunic for Jesus—looking after the chickens and the donkey, baking bread. No longer does Mary go to the well for water; Talitha does that. The gathering in the old kitchen at night is different now, but Mary's presence helps make up for her son's absence.

The older nephews are with Jesus, so there is no one to look after the fields. Men are hired to work them as sharecroppers. There is excitement in that small house when someone comes with news of Jesus: amazing miracles, conversions, people's admiration, new disciples, the first hints of trouble with the Pharisees and doctors of the Law.

One day Lazarus comes, pale and tired. He has to rest after arriving.

"Where's Jesus?" He wants to see him as soon as possible, get to know his disciples, see him preaching to the people. His sisters send affection and regards to Mary. When will Jesus come again to Bethany?

In the morning, Mary finds him still too weak to leave. As he eats listlessly, she tells him that people are so eager to listen to Jesus that some are now coming from very distant places.

"Mary, I will leave as soon as I can."

"Simon is here, you could go with him. Lazarus, wouldn't you like to become a disciple of Jesus?"

"I wish I could, Mary, with all my heart. I don't know what I could do with my life that would be better than that. But I'm not well enough, and I would be a hindrance. The disciples sleep in the fields if they must. I am his friend who loves him, serves him, and follows him in his mind's eye. But I do that at home, and it's there I believe that God wishes me to be sanctified."

Simon is not long in coming. He greets Mary affectionately.

"Jesus is close to Capernaum. The multitudes surround him everywhere. We hardly have time to eat."

"If you feel well, Lazarus, tomorrow we can go to see him. We will stop at Tiberias, at the house of Alphaeus and his family. I've known them a long time. Matthew, their son, is a childhood friend of Jesus."

"I know, Mary, Jesus has told me."

Early next morning they leave. Mary again rides the little donkey. Talitha also has come to see Jesus; Lazarus rides the mule with Simon walking at his side. When they reach the valley, others join them. The crowd grows as they get closer to the lake. The people are merry, although the sick ride with great difficulty. There are children, young men and women, the elderly, townspeople, mostly poor. There are peasants and shepherds; shopkeepers and artisans, sons of the God of Israel who want to see their Messiah. And, among them, modest and humble, like any other woman of her times, is Mary, his mother, wearing her recently washed old blue mantle.

The family at Tiberias receives them joyfully. Matthew is not among them. He has gone with Jesus. His wife, Veronica, explains that he went in order to follow the Master. A woman of faith, she is not troubled that her husband follows Jesus: God will not abandon her.

Other people join them at dawn, and they proceed toward Nain. Jesus is said to be there. With them are strangers from Syria, Tyre, Sidon, as well as Jews from Jerusalem and the Decapolis. At length they encounter an immense crowd that hinders their progress. Leaving the beasts behind, Simon clears a way, crying out that he is with Mary, the mother of Jesus. The people look at her and allow them to mount the hill with difficulty. From the summit John sees them coming, and, advancing, he takes Mary by the hand and leads her to a place where she can hear Jesus easily.

They sit on the dry grass. People fall silent, waiting quietly. Even the children look toward the Master as he, clad in white, his hair blown by the wind, begins to speak. His voice is strong and deep, a voice with authority. The crowd listens attentively.

"Blessed the poor in spirit . . ."

Mary's eyes are fixed on her son. Here is the Emmanuel, the Redeemer, of whom the angel spoke. How many years she waited for this moment as she watched him grow! "Oh Joseph, how you would love to be here with us! You planted; others reap!"

Motionless and enthralled, Lazarus listens. Curled at his feet, Tabitha sobs like a baby.

"Don't cry, daughter, be glad—salvation has come for all these peoples."

"Oh Jesus, I want to love you more every day."

Hours pass, the day draws to a close. Jesus dismisses the people. Coming down, he approaches his mother and briefly greets the group. Then he leaves, surrounded by the disciples, by followers, and by the sick, who shout in gratitude that God is close to his people.

❖ ❖ ❖

Mary is back in Nazareth. Jesus has left for Judea. Relatives and travelers bring news of his miracles and healings, his ardent words opening horizons of eternal life for souls, and the opposition of the self-styled learned ones. Mary reflects on it all, praying ceaselessly for him. She prays that people will understand his teaching, for they need him—even the indifferent or hostile ones. She accompanies him in her thoughts, while her hands work steadily.

Mary sends food and clothing those who go to hear him. Such details of affection are dictated by a love much like any mother's for an absent son.

One night James appears, wet and chilled, his hands reddened. He has a full beard. They summon Mary, who just then is with his mother. As he warms himself next to the fire, his tears fall. The women arrive.

"What is wrong, son?"

"What is the news of Jesus?"

"It's John. He has been put in prison. Although he is in awe of him, Agrippa is holding him prisoner in his fortress."

Mary fears for him. He is so passionate! He is sure to reproach the King for his misconduct.

Winter comes and goes, rainy and windy. In the spring there is news that Jesus is again in Galilee. Mary is eager to see him, but she fears distracting or troubling him by making him think she is sad without him. She needs him so much! But he is carrying out his mission, for which God sent him to the world, and nothing—not even her great love—could move her to get in its way.

But the nieces and nephews insist, especially Cleophas's youngest, who wants to go with him. Joseph remains in the workshop. His wife is expecting a child soon. They live in the small house adjacent to the workshop that formerly was Mary's. The young woman admires Mary greatly and is moved to see her knitting a tiny garment for her future child.

"If it is a boy, he will be called Joseph, like his father and his uncle, your husband, lady Mary. Joseph says he has not met a carpenter as good as he."

"That's true, daughter; he was a great artisan and a magnificent husband. Someday I will tell you about him."

Mary thinks about Joseph, and tears come to her eyes as she looks around that little house so full of memories.

They leave on a morning of foul weather threatening rain. Mary is eager to see her son yet at the same time does not want to interfere with his mission. The nieces and nephews are happy, unaware of her intimate feelings.

At Tiberias they ask for news of Jesus and then go to find him. Mary's emotion increases as they get closer. There are people with them, some from far away. At last they come to a village where a large crowd is listening to Jesus. Adobe walls that some people have scaled block him from their sight. They stop under a tree and listen for the familiar and beloved voice. Some fellow countrymen recognize them and open the way, but they cannot go very far. Word of Mary's presence reaches Jesus. He interrupts his discourse and turns toward them. He speaks words easily understood in their simple sense, but Mary understands the deeper meaning to perfection. But she remains where she is, one more among many, humble and attentive.

When Jesus finishes speaking, Peter and John approach; they greet the newcomers affectionately and invite them to stay where Jesus lodges.

The little house is surrounded by people, the sick and the healthy, neighbors and strangers. Jesus is waiting for them.

"Son, how wonderful to see you again."

"Mother, God be with you. Be welcome."

There is little for them to say. Her son is no longer hers. He belongs to these people anxious for his word, and to those who do not know him yet—to humankind. These now are his mother and brothers and sisters. Jesus rumples the hair of Mary of Cleophas's youngest son, now thirteen, and looks at him affectionately. The bolder cousins say good-bye with a kiss. The last to go, Mary does the same. John accompanies them some distance, telling them of Jesus's latest doings.

The winter, too, is rainy this year. News of Jesus is scarce in Nazareth. But it is rumored that some Jews want to seize him and say he breaks the commandments of the Law. He is not a Messiah according to their model.

One gray day Lazarus arrives numb and disheveled. He has lately been with Jesus until he retired to a secluded place. He brings bad news: Herod has had John killed. Mary throws up her hands in distress.

"Oh my John, my little John! What have they done to you? I held you when you were born, I watched you grow, I saw you play, heard you laugh with Jesus. John, my little one!"

Mary sobs, her face muffled in her mantle, next to the hearth whose light so often illuminated the youthful and loving face of John.

"Ungrateful King, with so much the Lord has given you. Your father sought to kill Jesus, and now you have killed John. God have mercy on you!"

Talitha weeps for John. She knew him only a little but admired him much. Lazarus stays some days in the house, keeping Mary company.

News still more alarming comes at the beginning of spring: Jesus is in danger. He has had to flee. His whereabouts are unknown.

"If the King has done this to John, whom he respected, what won't he do to Jesus if he will not bow to his whims? My God, look after him; watch over him. He is your beloved Son, but in the end he is a man of flesh and blood, who suffered when he heard of the death of John—John whom he loved as a brother. Lord, Your ways are unfathomable. I accept and love Your will!"

Mary determines to go to Bethany to be closer to Jesus. Mary of Cleophas accompanies her, wanting to see her sons who are with the Master and ready to share his fate. Passover is near. Pilgrims throng the roads. Mounted again on the humble donkey, Mary sets out on the road to the south in hopes of being with Jesus soon.

11

Time of Love, Time of Suffering

WHENEVER MARY HAS GONE TO JERUSALEM in the last few years, she has passed through Bethany, to the big old house—one of the few still standing since the wars of occupation—of Jesus's dear friends. Brimming with joy, the two sisters would come out to meet her, Martha the more reserved, Mary crying out happily. For them this was the year's high point. Lazarus saw to unloading and stabling the beasts, while the sisters hugged and kissed Mary and welcomed her into the house.

Mary enjoyed spending a few days with them. Her love was reciprocated there. They even kept a room ready—"Mary of Nazareth's" they called it. It was a large room on the upper floor, with white wooden floor boards polished by the tread of many footsteps in time, a small window just under the roof surrounded by a noble stone frame and looking out on fields of wheat, olive trees, and vineyards. In the distance lies the outskirts of Jerusalem behind the Mount of Olives. There was a modest bed to the right, and beside it furs from the big old chest placed there with care. To one side of the window, there was a washstand, legs resting on a base of black wood, and on it a jug of hot water.

Built into the center wall of the house was a chimney in which thickly wrapped adobe bricks were heated in bad weather before being placed at the foot of the bed to warm the sheets. They would also place a bunch of thyme in the room, knowing that Mary liked its smell. In this and other such details the sisters enjoyed pleasing Mary.

In springtime one heard the song of the turtledove nesting in the olive trees, in summer the sharp cry of the partridges, and almost always the chattering of swallows in the eaves. In a corner was a small loom formerly used by the sisters' mother and now worked by them and Mary on rainy days. When the weather was good, they would go out in the mornings to see the animals, feed the chickens, and go to a pond where hungry fish ate the breadcrumbs they tossed them.

On mild afternoons they would gather in the courtyard with their sewing. Mary worked quickly and well, with a perfection in her stitches that the sisters admired. At night they were joined by Lazarus, who never tired of hearing about Jesus, his friend, and listening to Mary, whose voice and visage recalled him. In the big kitchen by the fire's heat and light, they cooked the food. From hooks in the roof and wall hung fruits of the last harvest. Big stone jars with wooden lids held fresh water which they drew with a small heartwood dipper.

By the light of the fire and the oil lamps on the wall, the ever lovely, pale, and serene face of Mary captivated everybody there—old sharecroppers, trusted employees, servants who had been born there and there would die, visiting relatives. Seldom did Mary speak of intimate details concerning Jesus and herself, but pressed by the others, she would do so now and then, and tell them about the birth of Jesus, the flight to Egypt, the trips to Jerusalem with Joseph. As she spoke, the silence deepened and only the crackle of the flames occasionally interrupted her words.

◆ ◆ ◆

Several years have passed since Mary's last stay in Bethany. Much has happened that the brother and sisters know about, since Jesus has been with them several times: How, having left his home in

Nazareth, he is traveling the roads of Palestine preaching his doctrine of salvation. Not long ago he brought back to life Lazarus, who had died after a brief illness. Still overwhelmed, they continually give thanks to God. Now Jesus has left again, traveling with his disciples to the outskirts of Ephraim, at the edge of the desert, because the Jews of the Temple want to seize him.

In Nazareth, Mary received news of Lazarus' sickness from relatives returning from Jerusalem. She decides to visit him, to assist his sisters and perhaps see Jesus, who she knows is in that vicinity. Mary of Cleophas, her sister-in-law and good friend, offers to accompany her together with Jacob, one of her sons; the others are with Jesus.

They leave at dawn on a warm day when spring is near. Mary casts a last glance at her little house: so empty since her son left! She carries, well wrapped, the seamless tunic she has just finished making for Jesus. How many hours spent thinking about him as she wove threads she had spun while Ana was alive.

Talitha and Joseph say good-bye to them, making her think of her husband. They will care for the house and the animals. No longer do Joachim and Ana come out to see them off as they once did, for they have already passed on. And Jesus? It's been three years since he left. What is happening to him? There are rumors that some of the Jews want to seize him. As they set out the sun is already peeking between the mountains. The journey is uneventful, short, and often passed in silence.

They arrive at the house of the family in Bethany at dusk on the fourth day. Dogs bark. A delighted young girl hurries into the house to proclaim the arrival of Mary and her friend.

The sisters emerge rejoicing. They had not been expecting a visit from Mary, and now they cover her with kisses and hugs and tears of joy. Lazarus, pale and leaning on a walking stick, comes out and embraces her. "Jesus saved me, although I was dead. Now he is in Ephraim, for fear of the Jews."

They accompany her to her room and get a fire going in the fireplace. A little later all gather in the old kitchen, where they tell in great detail of the visit of Jesus and his disciples, the illness, death, and resurrection of Lazarus, Jesus's words to Martha, and the intrigues of the Jews. Mary retires early to rest from the long journey.

The days pass as on other occasions, filled with work, prayer, and kindness toward visitors from Jerusalem inquiring about the healing of Lazarus. Mary loves and is loved by that family with a sincere and spontaneous love.

The weather is still fresh. The first turtledoves sing in the olive trees, and the doves fuss in the courtyard. Flocks of starlings cross the blue sky. The field hands plow the surrounding fields, their oxen pulling ancient iron-tipped wooden plows, turning over the black soil softened by the first spring showers. There is no news of Jesus.

One day the afternoon stillness is interrupted by the arrival of a mule bearing an out-of-breath farm boy. "Jesus is coming with his disciples. They'll be here soon."

Mary's heart pounds. The sisters jump up from their sewing to prepare the house. Lazarus thanks God as he passes to and fro in the corridor. Now he can thank Jesus calmly for returning him to life. At last they can be seen beyond the gate. Jesus's figure stands out, tall, clad in white, treading with measured steps. They fling open the doors. Mary remains in the courtyard. The sisters hurry to the portico, where Jesus greets them. Lazarus embraces him with a sob he cannot restrain. They enter the house.

"Mother, are you here? Blessed be God!"

Mary embraces and kisses him in silence, serene. Jesus, her son, is well though thinner; his look is more profound. Mary of Cleophas hugs her sons with tears of joy. More people arrive; the courtyard fills up. More greetings, more talk. The sisters hurry about serving everyone. John joins Mary who sits on a bench next to the courtyard wall. He settles himself at her feet while she smoothes his hair.

"How you have grown, John! How is your mother, Salome? I saw her last in Cana of Galilee. Tell me where you have been."

"By Ephrem, on the edge of the desert, where John began to baptize. Out of envy the Temple Jews want to seize Jesus."

"Why have you come back?"

"Jesus wants to go to Jerusalem to give testimony and celebrate the Passover."

John's eyes are fixed on Mary. He doesn't know her well, but each time he loves her more. She looks so much like Jesus! Loving her, he loves the Master; for he discerns that between them there are bonds stronger than those binding any other mother and son.

"Lady Mary: why did you come so far?"

"I wanted to be with Jesus and with you. I have a feeling that something is going to happen to him. Just seeing him and listening to him for a few moments consoles me. John, you'll always be with him, won't you?"

"Yes, lady Mary, I'll never leave him. Peter and all the rest say the same."

"Tell me, John, why have you left home, parents, land, future, and followed Jesus?"

"My lady, Jesus captivated me from the moment I met him. His bearing, his voice, his gaze . . . but more than anything, his words. He speaks words of eternal life, love for God, and for all mankind. And then, he asked me to follow him. That was three years ago, beside the lake."

"One day you will understand more things, John. Do you know whose son he is?"

"Yes, lady Mary, yours and . . ."

"Yes, John, he is my son. And the son of God the Father. You will have to repeat that often when the time comes for it to be understood."

John looks at Mary with amazement and immense love, then takes her hand and kisses it. Tears fill his eyes. What greatness there is in Mary, yet she is so natural and modest.

Again she tousles his hair affectionately. Soon Jesus comes out with Lazarus and without haste warmly greets everybody. They then go in to dine. Martha and her sister serve. Lazarus reclines with Jesus among the disciples. Mary watches him and listens. Jesus gives thanks to God, and they sup with happy hearts. Tired from the journey, they retire soon after. Mary prays in her room, thankful to God because she is close to Jesus, because he is safe and sound, and because tomorrow she will again be with him.

◆ ◆ ◆

Sunrise brings a radiant spring day. Mary and the sisters have been working since early morning preparing food. John is the first to greet her and remains helping her. The rest settle down in the courtyard. Jesus arrives rested and dressed in fresh clothes. How much he is loved at Bethany! He greets his mother and eats breakfast beside her.

"Mother, I am going to Jerusalem. Openly, so that everyone can see me. Thank you for this new tunic."

They leave for the city. Happy and expectant, Mary and the other women follow. The sky is speckled by a few white clouds. Jesus walks steadily ahead and speaks little. On reaching Bethphage, before commencing the climb toward the Mount of Olives, he sends two disciples ahead to obtain a colt. They soon return with one and the pace slows. Some toss their cloaks on it and help Jesus mount. Others spread their mantles before him as he passes and shout in jubilation. A crowd gathers, for there are many pilgrims to Jerusalem on this road.

As the procession moves on, people begin to praise him in the words of Psalm 118. Mary remembers hearing those same words spoken by the shepherds and proclaimed by angels at his birth. She is glad at his reception and wonders what will happen now. Pharisees approach him, and he speaks calmly to them. They withdraw. At a bend of the road, Jerusalem can be seen through the trees white and shining against the mountains.

Jesus stops to look upon the city. The procession halts, and the children who had been running beside it draw near. A breeze stirs Jesus's hair and ruffles his robes. People are silent. They see tears in his eyes, his look troubled as he speaks of the destruction of that city, so mighty in their eyes, as punishment for rejecting him. Mary listens closely to these words. Once again she feels dark forebodings that the celebratory mood of this day cannot dispel. When Jesus resumes his progress, the people happily resume their praises. They cut palm branches to strew before him, joined now by people from the city who have heard of his coming.

As they draw near to the temple, Mary worries that soldiers may come to seize him. When they arrive, she is amazed to see Jesus dismount and begin to expel the merchants and money changers. There is a commotion—some approving, others disapproving. From a distance she sees him addressing the crowd, but she can hardly hear him. She only knows that Jesus, her Jesus, handsome and serene, is heard admiringly by those people avid for God's word.

In the afternoon she returns to Bethany with the women, happy and praising God: Jesus has triumphed over the doctors of the Law and Pharisees! The people welcomed him and listened to him with gladness!

At night, Jesus comes with his disciples, tired and contented. He sits next to her in the kitchen and eats what they bring him.

"Mother, how long are you staying?"

"As long as you are here, son."

Mary stays in Bethany on the days Jesus goes to Jerusalem with his followers. She waits for him to return in the evening, with the house tidy and cleaned and a fire in the hearth lit. If he does not come that night, the next day John tells everything they have done. He speaks of growing crowds that listen to him, the resentment of the men of the temple, foreigners who have come from afar and want to meet him and talk to him. He recounts his prophecies.

On the third day, Jesus does not go to Jerusalem. Everyone stays in Bethany. The morning is fresh. Rain has fallen during the night, and early buds are sprouting on the trees. Jesus is happy, as are the disciples. Mary and the sisters serve simple fare, and they eat in friendship and harmony. Then they all go for a walk in the fields, as a family might. Mary and Jesus walk hand in hand, while John, wide-eyed, can't get enough of watching both. They walk slowly on the wide, earthen path among olive and carob trees. Nearby a sower is tossing wheat seed into newly turned furrows. Behind him comes a youth who closes each furrow with a small mule-drawn plow. Thus the seed will die in order to bear fruit.

Mary is happy to have Jesus near. It has been a long time since she walked holding his hand like this. How much has happened! Lazarus tells Jesus about the farm. When they pass some houses, a frightened hen darts in front of them and, summoning her chicks, gathers them under her wings. Arriving at a mustard tree, they sit down in its shade. Jesus talks with a few people. A group from Jerusalem approaches. Everyone wants to be with the Master, hear him, and be looked upon by those deep eyes so like his mother's.

Some sheep are grazing nearby; the shepherd, with his dog close by, watches lest they wander into the planted fields. In his worn clothing and tangled hair, with his crook in hand, he approaches Jesus and stares at him; the Master speaks to him affectionately and asks about his flocks. People from nearby hamlets arrive; the crowd grows. Mary is happy to see how much her son is loved by these simple folk—people of the sort who have suffered so much over the centuries.

It is pleasant to be close to Jesus, and time speeds by. At last they head back to the farm. Simon the leper is waiting for them there. He has come with a reminder of the invitation to dine at his house that day; it will be a great honor for him. Jesus greets him warmly and promises they will leave soon. Mary goes to the kitchen where, as on other occasions, Martha has remained bustling about. Together with her sister and other young women, she helps arrange what they will take. They are happy and talkative; the atmosphere is festive. Yet Mary senses that the days ahead will be very different.

Simon's house is a short distance from Lazarus's. Large and well furnished, it has an ample sitting room with a beamed ceiling. A large table has been set there, and they promptly arrange themselves around it. Jesus and Simon preside; the disciples and

Lazarus are next to him. Mary is at one end with the women of the house. Martha helps serve. Before the meal, Mary, her sister, approaches Jesus humbly and, breaking open a container of aromatic nard, pours it over the Master. Back in her place, she offers a small quantity of the perfume that remains to Mary, who gently rejects it but thanks her for the loving gesture. The intense aroma fills the house. Everyone knows what has happened. Judas protests; Mary, hearing him, is overwhelmed by Jesus's response: his anointing, his burial. What Jesus foretells always comes to pass. What will happen? She sees Judas leave surreptitiously. Never has she trusted his fawning manner and today, least of all, his shifty gaze.

The supper ends. There is a sense of foreboding. Jesus leaves with his disciples. Mary remains with the sisters and Simon's family helping to straighten up. As the first stars appear, they return to the house of Lazarus. The weather is cold, and the moon is out. They walk in silence, praying, until dogs start a racket as they reach the house. Mary withdraws to her room and prays by the light of the fire.

"My Lord, My God, protect Jesus, Your Son and mine. See how he works for You; he doesn't rest. I remember him when he was little—coming in from the fields with Joseph, clothes full of the smell of hay and smiling as he came to kiss me. How much he is loved by some! I have seen them hanging onto his words, their hearts in their hands. But others do not love him, because they don't truly love You, Lord. They love their traditions and their readings of Your law better. I have seen hatred in their eyes. I am frightened lest they rise up against him, lest they wound and kill . . . their God."

The fire slowly dies out. A steady rain outside the window summons her to sleep. The house is silent.

A gorgeous day dawns, heralding the coming spring. Mary hears the song of linnets in a tree nearby. Beyond the olive trees clothed in silver by the first rays of the sun the white walls of Jerusalem lie before her. Mary prays again, looking at the city where Jesus is going.

"Lord, what will happen today? Don't take him so soon! We need him. My heart shudders at the thought of something befalling him. All the years I looked after him, all the nights I watched over his sleep when he was a baby. How often I carried him in my arms, dried his tears, fed him, clothed him. To me Jesus will always be my little one. If only there were some way I could protect him. My Lord and my God, I accept Your will; guard Your Son."

The sisters, happy and talkative, come to tell her they have prepared a simple hamper. She smiles and lets herself be kissed by them. Jesus is downstairs with Lazarus. He is very serious yet calm.

"Good morning, Mother, God be with you."

"May He accompany you, my Jesus. I prayed contemplating Jerusalem and speaking to God about what you said yesterday. Your words quite overcame me."

Peter and the others begin arriving. They greet Jesus. John comes to her and receives a kiss on his tousled hair. They talk and laugh while they eat; sometimes they are silent. Jesus tells Peter and John to go in advance and prepare everything for the Paschal supper that night. He names the house where it will be celebrated. Rising, he invites Mary to dine at the home of Mark's mother. Then he leaves.

Mary remains with Mary of Cleophas, the two sisters, and other young women. They clear the table, at the same time chattering about how they will help Mark's mother at that Paschal supper, for many will be there. Mary spends the morning working in the big kitchen. She is uneasy, wanting to be alone, her thoughts constantly with God, her heart with Jesus.

"What is going to happen to him?" In early afternoon John arrives announcing that everything is ready. She gets ready to leave with the women, who bear the hot food on trays.

Jesus goes behind the women with his disciples; all carry walking sticks. The road and the hill of the Olives that just a few days before they climbed joyfully seems steep and difficult to Mary now. Rain clouds now and then cover the sun. Many pilgrims join the group, some watching them curiously. Mary expects to see a squad of armed men emerge to arrest Jesus. Close to the stream called the Cedron, they come to the first houses. Some onlookers gather, while others hurry by. The children play in the streets, unaware of their elders' doings.

A flock of sheep and lambs being taken to the temple blocks the way; they will be sacrificed tomorrow. Unaware of that, they hurry along at the urging of shepherd's cries. Jesus and his companions reach the house where Peter and others await them, and they all enter. Jesus greets Mark's mother, Mary, and with the disciples goes to the second floor where they enter the room that has been prepared. Already it is lighted. Hanging on the smooth white walls are rustic ceramic adornments.

In the center of the room is a great table. To the side is another smaller table bearing containers of food as well as jars, towels, and clay vessels. Mary seats herself on a simple bench against the wall. With her are the other women. Some young men beside them sit on the floor. On the table are serving dishes with roasted pieces of the lamb that Peter and John sacrificed at the temple that morning. John, the youngest present, asks Jesus to explain the religious meaning of this supper. Jesus does so in measured tones. When he finishes, they sing hymns.

Jesus takes a piece of meat without salt or seasoning and eats it with unleavened bread. His disciples do the same in silence. Mary receives a small fragment wrapped in bitter herbs. They drink from goblets and sing a hymn in grave tones. Jesus also sings. Mary remembers teaching him to sing as a child. They used to sing with Joseph, so long ago. Thanks are given to God. Outside the window there is darkness and the barely audible hum of the city can be heard. A gust of wind shakes the lamp's flames: the presence of the Father is felt.

Jesus sets aside his walking stick, comes to the small table, and washes his hands in the basin. The disciples do the same. Jesus looks fondly at Mary and those beside her, then awaits the disciples at the table as they return there. Taking up the pitcher, the wash basin, and some towels, he goes to the disciples.

Kneeling, he gestures to one to put his feet forward for washing. Conversation ceases, and all wait to see what he will do. In silence, Jesus washes to the feet of each in turn. Only Peter objects; Jesus responds. When he reaches Judas, the disciple lowers his eyes and nervously grasps the table.

Mary is filled with joy and tenderness at what her son is doing. She sees several weeping silently at seeing their Master at their feet. When he finishes, he sets down the utensils and towels beside her, returns to the center of the table, and resumes his place next to John.

The women bring them supper, pour more wine into the goblets, put bread in the baskets, and serve the food that was prepared with painstaking care. Jesus takes a mouthful, sips the wine and looking at them calmly; he speaks while they eat. All is still inside and outside the house as if the angels, indeed all of nature, desired to share in this outpouring of Jesus's love upon his friends. He speaks of their love for one another, reflecting his love for each of them, of their union with him, and tells them not to fear rejection by the world. Time seems to stop; all eyes are on Jesus—except those of Judas staring fixedly at the table. Mary Magdalene sobs in a corner. Other women raise handkerchiefs to their eyes.

Jesus rises, and the disciples do the same, but he tells them to remain where they are. The silence is interrupted only by the sputtering of the candles, and in this profound silence, soul speaks to soul. Jesus gazes quietly at them. He must leave, and he wants to stay; he loves them and through them loves all mankind. Taking loaves from the basket, he gives one to each and pronounces words that Mary hears clearly. They eat in spiritual absorption. Then, taking the pitcher, he pours wine into their cups and speaks clear and overwhelming words. They drink slowly, meditatively. With a grim expression and mumbled good-bye, Judas leaves. The disciples whisper among themselves as he hastens down the stairs. Seeing him leave, Mary sighs. The atmosphere lightens with him gone.

Jesus reclines again and resumes speaking of the New Commandment—the supreme law of love—of the Holy Spirit, of the dwelling he has prepared for them in his Father's house. His love, that immense love that Mary knows so well, extends to God's own will and to the handful of people listening to him and looking on with shining eyes. Now his words become a farewell. He rises as does everyone else. Donning his cloak, he goes to Mary and kisses her:

"Mother, don't worry about me. Watch over these others who need you. God be with you."

He thanks Mark's mother for the meal and leaves, preceded by his disciples, telling Mary as he goes: "We are going to the Garden of Olives."

The women remain. Mary helps clean up, but her thoughts are elsewhere. Jesus has said good-bye. What will become of him? Mark's mother accompanies her to her room, tidy and dark, whose only light comes from a small lamp in the corner and from the bright night sky seen through a high window. It is hot. Having no wish for sleep, she prays.

"My Lord and my God, Holy Father, watch over Jesus; I sense that his end is near. He has fulfilled his mission. But he is so young! He has been among his own for such a short time. How much he loves them! He gave them his body in the bread. And they—how much they love him! They are willing to give their lives for him. Lord, look after him, he is Your Son. The men of the temple cannot bear him. And what wrong has he done? He has taught so many to love You more, with a genuine love. Others he has healed. And he has filled everybody with hope. I wonder why he went at this hour to the garden? Tomorrow will he go to go to the temple? Lord, I am Your handmaid. May Your will be done."

In the silence of the night a cock's crow is heard far off, close to the palace.

❖ ❖ ❖

Daybreak is cloudy. With Mark's mother, Mary joins the other women. The signs of sleeplessness are on their faces. The weather changes, a gusty wind blows, and there is an odor of wet earth. John and James arrive, looking distraught. Their clothes are wet.

"They have taken Jesus. It happened at midnight in the garden. Judas betrayed him. Jesus asked that we be let go. Then we fled; we left him alone. Later Peter and I went to the house of Annas, and from there they took him to the palaces of the high priest and of Herod. Now they are taking him to the Praetorium, to Pilate. They want him to pronounce a death sentence. Oh, Mary! What wrong has Jesus done?" John sobs as he drinks hot broth and eats a piece of bread.

"John, I'll go with you to Jesus."

"Lady, there is much hatred toward him. They are stirring up people to go to the Praetorium and support their accusations. I fear they will try to harm you."

"No, John, nobody will harm me. I will go with the other women, poor mothers like me."

Joined by the other women, Mary wraps herself in her mantle and leaves, with John going ahead. It is bright daylight, with clouds dotting the sky. People hurry past on their way to the temple. Two men are speaking loudly. "They have arrested Jesus the man from Galilee, and taken him to the Praetorium, to Pilate. He wouldn't speak to Herod!"

Mary goes faster. The streets begin to fill up; everyone is heading to the great plaza before the Praetorium. They barely find a place on the edge of the crowd, beside a wall that provides them with shade. The crowd is made up mostly of men. A stone's throw away are some steps going up to a terrace. And there is Jesus . . . standing alone, hands bound, a small red cape, torn and dirty, over his shoulders, his clothing stained with blood, a crown of thorns upon his head, his bruised face furrowed by threads of blood; still he is serene, in full command of himself. The procurator, Pilate, dressed in Roman garb, approaches him, surrounded by guards. Between Jesus and the people are the priests and their servants. Appearing haggard from lack of sleep, they accuse him viciously while stirring up the rabble, who, confused and prompted, shouts: "Crucify him, crucify him!"

For Mary the words are like a sword that pierces her heart. The interrogation of Jesus continues, while the Jews keep up their accusations. The people become increasingly aroused.

"My God, let what these people are shouting not be taken into account! Take pity on Your Son, Lord, mistreated as he is!"

The voices of the priests and the shouts of the people go on, although some of the onlookers are frightened and silent. John wants to shield her from hearing those voices and he wants to do something for Jesus, too. He shouts out in his defense.

Pilate re-enters the Praetorium with Jesus. There is a moment of tense silence. It is midday. Pilate sits, leaving Jesus to stand before the Jews. At last Pilate demands silence, but it is long in coming, so worked up are they! Now he pronounces his sentence: "Let him be crucified!"

A murmur, like the sound of crashing rocks being dragged by a storm-driven river, runs through the crowd. It reaches Mary, who shudders inwardly yet remains serene, her eyes moist but no more; not so her friends, who burst into sobs. John shouts—"He is innocent!"—but the noise of the rabble drowns out his words.

Mary watches them snatch the red cape from Jesus and restore his robes. They untie his hands so that he can don them, and finally his tunic, the one she began so lovingly in the house in Nazareth upon their return from Cana, seamless, whose threads were from the days when she spun with Ana, while Joseph labored in the workshop and Jesus helped while the pigeons fluttered in the courtyard. She cries: "Oh, my son, what will they do to you?"

Soldiers bring crossed beams to the foot of the steps, shoving two men with them. A voice murmurs at her side, "They are thieves!" Jesus slowly descends the steps, and again there is silence. They lift the cross onto his back. The two thieves protest and are beaten. A procession forms, mounted soldiers at its head and other soldiers on foot behind the condemned men. They can barely make their way through the crowd surging around them. A voice shouts: "They are being taken to Golgotha through the Gate of Judgment!"

Mary leaves the plaza with John and the women, intending to station herself to see Jesus go by and, if at all possible, to accompany him, but it is hard to get through the people rushing back and forth before them. The sun is brutal. They come up on another group of women, among them John's mother, who joins them. At last they reach a street where already many people are waiting impatiently. The procession comes around a bend: Jesus is last, with the heavy cross on his shoulders and the crown of thorns still on his head. As he passes by, he sees his mother and gazes at her. Mary cannot suppress a sob of pain at seeing him so disfigured, his bruised face so bloody. If she could, she would heal him by her look, console him by her presence. They maneuver through the crowd and come to where Jesus is, but the soldiers force them back with their lances. John shouts: "She is the mother of Jesus!"

Those rough men hesitate and allow them to remain behind them. The march continues through those narrow, slippery, now tightly packed streets leading toward the Old Gate.

Exhausted, Jesus staggers, then he falls onto his knees. The procession halts. Some laugh. The executioners grow irritated. A man coming toward them carrying a load of vegetables on his shoulders is forced to take the cross of Jesus. Then Jesus looks at the women who are following him with Mary and feel pity for him. He speaks to them for several moments. But then, still helped by that man, he resumes the march amid a growing crowd. Some people scream at Jesus, others rebuke the Roman soldiers, and most look on with a mix of curiosity and amazement. Veronica, Matthew's wife, steps forward boldly and wipes his face with a white cloth.

Now the sun beats down mercilessly while black clouds gather on the horizon. The cortege is joined by people who rush to see him close at hand. A crucifixion is an impressive spectacle that stirs conflicting feelings in onlookers: compassion for the executed, dislike for the executioners.

On the outskirts of the city, a small hillock, bare and sinister, rises at the side of the road. At its foot the man who has helped carry the cross takes his leave. Accepting the burden, Jesus drags himself almost to the summit behind the thieves. The soldiers, agitated and impatient, pull him the rest of the way. Mary and the women approach until the guards stop them. Jesus waits patiently. Some women of Jerusalem come with jars of wine mixed with myrrh and give it to the executioners, who, with contempt, offer the wine to those condemned. Jesus barely tastes it.

Mary watches them rip away his clothing. He is shoved to the cross lying on the ground and stretches out his arms on that wood. Mary hears the deafening sound of the hammer driving nails into his calloused carpenter's hands and his feet. The blows pierce her to the heart. Then the men nail a notice on the top of the cross, and raise it, with Jesus hanging from it, until it drops into an open hole into which they heap stones to steady it.

Nailed to his cross, Jesus is exposed there to everyone's view. The sun scorches his face. Soon the thieves' crosses rise on either side of him. The indifferent executioners pick up their tools and the clothing of the condemned men to divide among themselves. Mary watches them throw dice for the tunic she had given Jesus a short time ago.

The guards and the mounted soldiers retire to one side, the horses pawing the ground restlessly as though uneasy at the cruelly spilled blood gushing down the beams and dripping on the ground. Down the slope the rabble mutter and grow ever more rebellious.

Priests, scribes, and temple attendants arrive. The crowd behind them surges forward to hear what they say to Jesus. At once nervous and sneering, they laugh and shout at him. Mary and John want to cry out: "You have already condemned him— now let him die in peace!"

The women also come close, and the soldiers let them, there no longer being any danger of their trying to save the crucified one: he is nearing death. Seated, lances between their knees, the soldiers watch the people surrounding the veiled woman who is the mother of one of the condemned. "Poor woman! What could her son have done to end like this?"

They stand a few steps from the crosses. John is pale, eyes large and round, making his face more like a child's. They hear Jesus ask the Father to forgive those who crucified him—precious words that make them weep silently. Mary can see her son close at hand.

"My God, how wounded he is!"

His knees bleed, his sides, his hands, his feet, his head, which he turns to fix his eyes upon her. Mary lifts her eyes to him and their looks meet: divine eyes of Jesus, profound and most kind, eyes she saw first in Bethlehem and, shining like stars, for so many years in Nazareth, now reddened and half-shut amid bruises. Jesus asks her to take John as her son, and John, who is standing behind her, to take her as his mother. John takes her hand and kisses it amid tears; Mary only says: "John, son."

Jesus says he is thirsty. Mary and the women want to give him something to drink. Knowing it isn't allowed, they plead, and a soldier rises and, grumbling, finds a broken stalk on which he fixes a sponge soaked in sour wine, then raises it to him while the others joke; Jesus barely tastes it and refuses it. Again he lowers his head on his wounded chest.

Time cuts like a knife through that divine yet human scene. One of the thieves rebukes him, in his anguish and pain not knowing what he says. The other one responds to him, then turns toward Jesus, who looks at him and speaks to him. A woman near the man weeps for him—his wife, perhaps? Mary looks at her tenderly and consoles her with a few words. Jesus lowers his head again. It seems as if he hasn't the strength to raise it—until he does lift it toward the sky now starting to darken, and calls upon God the Father. It is a cry of anguish, from his humanity, fastened by exceedingly painful nails to a cross, before people who relish the spectacle. Now in the deepening darkness nature, itself moans. Mary hears him and prays to God for him; she knows well that the Lord is present there, does not abandon him, but permits this agony of His beloved Son so as to open the doors of heaven again for mankind.

The darkness increases. People who had stayed behind start to become frightened and flee. So do the priests and scribes. The soldiers become restless and wrap themselves in their mantles against the cold. Only the women and John remain with Mary, no other disciples or friends.

Jesus speaks again: Everything is complete. The people at the base of the hill are suddenly silent, the soldiers speechless. A light wind brushing Jesus's hair is the only thing that moves. It drowns the sobs of the inconsolable Mary Magdalene. Jesus takes a breath and, crying out, delivers his spirit to God the Father. His head drops onto his chest. He is dead. Suddenly an earthquake shakes the earth as if protesting the injustice of men that killed their God. Mary stands at the foot of the cross. The soldiers move away terrified. The centurion approaches on his skittish horse to make sure Jesus has died and speaks of faith as he does.

The few people who had remained run away now, terrified and begging God's forgiveness. The earth's tremors diminish until it is quiet. Timid sunlight scatters the mist surrounding them. A little over three hours have elapsed since they crucified him. Once again Jesus appears in all his greatness. The lifeless body is pale, but looking at it they do not see a corpse. For them he still is Jesus.

The thieves writhe in agony. The lengthening shadows of the crosses extend farther downhill in the light of the setting sun, down to the path on which some perspiring temple Jews are climbing with a message from the procurator in hand. They hand it nervously to the centurion while looking at the lifeless Jesus on the cross. Seated on his horse, he reads it, then orders the soldiers to break the legs of the crucified men, a cruel spectacle witnessed by Mary and those with her. Poor women, how much useless suffering! Coming to Jesus, one of the soldiers hesitates, looks toward Mary who is watching him, puts aside the hammer, and with his lance opens his side. Another painful trial for Mary, who shudders as if the lance had penetrated her own heart.

The servants of the priests are satisfied: Jesus is no longer a threat; they go back content. Soon the thieves die, and the women with them weep. There is a changing of the guard, but before leaving, the centurion passes close by Mary and pauses, looking at her thoughtfully.

Moments of silence follow, interrupted only by the sounds of the nearby city, which is preparing for the feast. Families gather in their homes, amid fires and lights to celebrate the Paschal supper. Mary wraps herself in her mantle. They bring her something to eat, but she cannot even taste it; barely a sip of water passes her dry lips. She prays and remembers.

"My God, Your Son has died on this cross for us. What has happened, Lord? Did it have to be like this? That good old man of the temple, Simeon, prophesied that a sword would pierce my heart because of this son. How that is true, Lord! The sword still pierces my side. If only I could have suffered for him. How much he has endured! Now he rests. Look at his face, how serene! What have these people done with Your Son? Why didn't they want to acknowledge him? They could have seen their God by just looking in his eyes."

Some swallows, the year's first, hover chirping over the crucified. The sun goes down behind the mountains. It is evening. Two men followed by attendants come up slowly, their robes blowing in the wind. They deliver an order to the sentries, who permit them to approach the crosses. Upon seeing Jesus illumined by the last rays of the sun they fall on their knees and pray in silence. Then they rise and tell Mary who they are. They will take Jesus from the cross and bear him to a sepulcher before nightfall. The helpers bring up ladders, pliers, and ropes. How difficult it is to pull the nails from that still-green wood!

Helped by Joseph of Arimathea, they carefully lower Jesus into Mary's arms. She kisses him quietly and closes his eyes with tenderness, while John and Nicodemus remove the crown of thorns with difficulty. Wrapping the body in a big linen cloth, they carefully carry him down the hill. The crosses above stand silhouetted against the sky, mute testimony to the tragedy. They reach the nearby orchard and the sepulcher. Joseph and the servants draw back the heavy stone covering its entrance. Mary, Nicodemus, John, and the women embalm Jesus's body with myrrh and aloes that spread their perfume over those darkened fields. They place him upon a large sheet that covers him and wrap him quickly with it. Mary gazes upon him for the last time by the light of candles. He is pale and peaceful, with the imprints of blows reminders of his passion. They place him at the rear of the sepulcher, then replace the heavy stone over the entrance.

They leave, walking by torchlight with the first stars starting to show. At the road leading up the hill of the crucifixion, the crosses can be seen glowing faintly in the moonlight. Nearby, Jerusalem sparkles with light and celebrates the feast, indifferent as it is to that group returning with heavy hearts and unwavering conviction: He will live.

12

$\mathcal{A}$ Bright Star in the Night

DAYS OF PRAYER AND RUMORS. Mary stays quietly at Mark's house with the women keeping her company. The disciples respect her pain and admire her integrity, simplicity, and supernatural outlook. Here is the strength that keeps her from lamenting and allows her to maintain her composure. She smiles at everyone and speaks to them calmly. They pray together, the others feeling the power of the love of God that flows from her.

Frequently it rains during the night, watering the new shoots that break through the earth announcing spring. Pilgrims begin returning to their countries. Most of the disciples remain hidden out of fear of the Jews. Their cowardice and their confusion still leave a bitter taste in their mouths. It was all so sudden!

Jesus is no longer at their side. It is not yet Sunday when Mary Magdalene, Mary of Cleophas, and Salome, wrapped in their mantles on account of the cold, faces covered to their eyes, arrive. Mary, who rose much earlier, receives them affectionately.

"Let's go to anoint Jesus."

Mark's wife becomes alarmed.

"Will the soldiers let you? And even if they do, who will move the heavy entrance stone for you?"

"God will provide, Mary. On seeing us, women of their own nation, maybe they will pity us. They are country people. Are you coming with us, Mary?"

"No, you go. God be with you. Tell me when you come back what you have seen."

Mary remains thoughtful; John stays at home like a faithful son who does not want to leave her alone. The minutes go by as slowly as the sun rises behind the mountains. The city awakens lazily with its characteristic noises. Mary's prayer springs up spontaneously: "My Lord and my God, Your son—where is he? Oh, when will I see his face again, hear his voice, tend his wounds? Jesus, my son, what they did to you! Great is your love for all, even those who crucified you, as mine is for you, growing as your absence grows longer. Where are you, son? Have you gone back to the Father already? That ungrateful cross does not leave my mind—harsh price for the rescue. How much it cost you to redeem the world! Are your wounds still bleeding? My pious friends have gone to anoint you again."

Sunrise. There is a faint sound, as of angel's wings. It is silent. Seated at the window, Mary looks toward the door. Jesus is there. Her Jesus, her beloved son, crucified two days before. Dead and buried, now he is alive, with the gentle look that conquers her soul.

"Son of my heart, you returned to the Father. Thank you for having come!"

Jesus does not speak. It is only a fleeting but clear vision, leaving Mary's heart comforted. Her eyes glitter with tears of gratitude. It is the same Jesus, her son!

The household wakes up. There are sounds of people moving about. Mark's wife, her friend, knocks at the door, then enters softly.

"Mary, your eyes are full of light, yet the sun has scarcely risen."

"Woman, today is a great day that will be remembered by all generations."

Hardly talking, they go down to the big kitchen for a simple breakfast. Mary, her gaze remote, accepts with thanks whatever is served her. As they clear the table, there is a pounding at the door. Mary and Salome rush in, excited and joyful.

176

"Jesus has risen! He is not in the tomb. The stone had been moved aside, and we found angels inside. They told us Jesus had risen and that he would go before us to Galilee. We were frightened, but we believed. Then they showed us the shroud and the wrappings. Magdalene did not want to return with us but she stayed there instead. Mary, your son has overcome death! He told us he would rise on the third day. How foolish we were not to believe him and instead go there to anoint his body."

Mark's mother cries joyfully and hugs Mary.

"Mary, now we will see him again. Blessed be God."

The morning hours pass slowly. Then Magdalene arrives, joyfully saying she has seen Jesus. He spoke to her in his familiar voice. "Lady, my heart is still pounding! It happened near the sepulcher where I had left Mary and Salome. The morning light was very clear, though my eyes were misty with tears that I could not contain. There was no one near, neither soldiers nor disciples. Suddenly I saw a man and asked him if he had seen Jesus being taken away. And it was he! My Lord. He spoke words of great comfort to my heart. Jesus, our Jesus, is alive! He told me he would return to the Father, our Father, our God, and then disappeared from sight. I remained staring in astonishment at the place where he had been, giving thanks to God. Then I began running. On the way I met Peter and John who were going to the tomb, and I told them about Jesus, and they started to run there; I hope they will be here soon."

The women exclaim excitedly, while Mary in her heart gives thanks to God and speaks with her son.

Peter, John, and several disciples arrive. They tell of their visit to the tomb. Magdalene recounts what she saw. Despite all, they are skeptical. They want so much to see Jesus again— why hasn't he appeared to them? Mary comforts them, assuring them they will soon see her son.

"Lady, do you believe so? Is it possible he has risen? Might not the Pharisees have taken him somewhere else for fear of us?"

"Have faith. Let us pray in the room where we had supper with him the last time."

Mary and Jesus's disciples pray—confident and fervent prayers, interrupted by frequent sobs, that become quiet as the afternoon fades. The walls of nearby buildings are reddened by the setting sun. More disciples come, asking about Jesus. They pray and gaze at Mary or speak of their sorrow at the death of her son. News spreads of the visits to the empty tomb and the visions. Hope mingles with their pain and doubt.

Peter steps into the courtyard, his eyes reddened, his bearing downcast. They leave him alone for some moments. Jesus appears clearly to him. Peter weeps—tears of pain, shame, and gratitude: "Jesus, my Master, you know I love you."

He re-enters the room, his expression radiant and head held high. All eyes turn to him. He tells Mary in a strong voice that Jesus has appeared to him. A murmur of surprise and happiness passes through the room.

Voices at the door, hurried footsteps rushing up the stairs. It is two disciples who during the afternoon had set off sadly for their village, Emmaus. Now they enter the room and happily report that Jesus appeared to them on the road and they recognized him in the breaking of the bread. Smiling, they hug their brothers, who share their joy. The oil lamps are lit, disclosing both doubt and certainty in the little group. There is a sound like the beating of angel's wings. Mary recognizes it. The voices fall silent, and suddenly there is Jesus at the center of the room—Jesus with a beautiful, shining face, speaking in his familiar voice, eyes full of love for these men who abandoned him, the lance wound in his side now visible.

Confusion and immense peace mingle in them. Still they are silent, expectant, uncertain. Jesus speaks to them, shows his hands and the wounds of the nails in his feet. Amazement gradually gives way to happiness among the onlookers. Truly he has risen!

Jesus goes to the table and eats some fish as so often he has done in Galilee. Now they firmly believe it is Jesus, their Jesus. He who was with them here at supper, then seized before their eyes in the orchard; all see and hear him except Thomas, who is absent, and Judas. He speaks to them as he did so often in the last three years, confirming them in faith with stirring words that open their minds to understand the Scriptures and all that happened. Rising, he tells them to go out and preach to all peoples what they have seen and heard. Mary, eyes fixed on her son and not missing a word, wants to embrace him. But now he disappears as he came, leaving them all with a happy silence soon broken by words and embraces. John approaches, his face flushed.

"Mother, blessed be God! The same Jesus is among us again. We will never be alone. We have him. We have you."

❖ ❖ ❖

The days pass. Disciples continue coming to that old house whose doors are generously open to all who wish to follow Jesus. The feast concludes, and the visitors begin to leave. Mary and the women prepare to go to Galilee to meet Jesus. Peter and John will go with them, while other disciples will join them on the way.

At sunset everyone gathers with Mary to pray. The high-ceilinged room has become the first domestic church. Mary speaks little and listens to everyone. Many come there to meet the mother of Jesus. She begins to feel their affection—her heart embraces them—and pours out love for the first disciples of her son. Among them, Stephen, exalted and passionate, stands out. He weeps as he speaks to the mother of his pain at the death of his beloved Master, her son.

"Would that I could have met you, Lady Mary, at a less painful moment. Without Jesus, we are sheep without a shepherd. May I go with you to Galilee? I want to see the Master's house."

"You may, Stephen. We will leave early on the second day of the week."

On Sunday, all of them, including Thomas, have been together there since morning. Mary is delighted to see them joyful, talking about the trip. Jesus has said he will go before them, so she will also see him again. Joy, intense and profound, fills her heart, thinking of that encounter.

At the time of prayer, they notice something in that big room where they are gathered behind locked doors. They become aware of a presence among them and fall silent. Jesus appears again, his face beautiful, his tunic resplendent. He approaches Thomas, who falls to his knees. Jesus reproaches him for his lack of faith. He shows his wounded hands and his side opened by the lance while addressing him with affection and firmness. He gazes at Mary for a moment before disappearing. They are elated, talkative, full of faith and confidence: the Master is still among them. At dawn they set out for the north country. Everyone gathers at the Door of Damascus. They are a picturesque and various group: villagers on poor mounts, Mary riding on the little donkey, other women along as well. John is a little distance behind her. Restless, Stephen soon joins them; Mary kindly answers some questions they ask her but still does not talk about her family life with Jesus. That will come at its proper moment.

John, who understands Mary's silence, speaks of Holy Scripture and the prophecies about Jesus. Stephen knows these to perfection; John is inspired and interprets the controversial points. Mary briefly underscores the citations, thereby enthralling the disciples. Peter and the others occasionally gather to hear the discussion. But she is discreet and quiet and lets them talk. Listening to Mary or observing her so dignified and lovely on her poor mount, Stephen grows ever more amazed and admires her more.

"John, Jesus told you to be for Mary as a son and she for you as your mother. Couldn't I also take her as mother?"

"Stephen, all of us who follow Jesus with sincere hearts are his children and hers."

Mary intervenes: "How did you meet him, Stephen?"

"It was at the beginning. I was with John the Baptist when he started to baptize. Later I met Jesus on his return from Galilee. I observed him very closely, but I did not decide. I came back again to follow him and listen to his words of eternal life. I was full of love for him, but—coward that I am—I did not decide to leave everything. One day, though, I saw how a young man whom Jesus had invited to follow him went away sadly because he possessed much wealth and lacked the generosity to leave it. Since then, I have abandoned everything I owned and joined the novices. With them, I witnessed the marvels worked by Jesus."

"Were you rewarded, Stephen, for leaving parents and lands to follow Jesus?"

"Jesus pays well, my Lady—a hundred to one and eternal life."

Halfway on the journey, they arrive at Sychar, where they stop at Jacob's well beside the road. Mary sits down on the ledge beside the well, enjoying the shade of an old mustard tree with new spring leaves. Cicadas sing loudly. The disciples stretch out to rest under the shade. A woman comes to draw water from the well. As she does, she studies Mary.

"Are you a Galilean? Are you going back to your land?"

"Yes, that is where we are going."

"Tell me, lady, what happened to Jesus the prophet? Pilgrims passing through say he was crucified."

"That is so, woman."

"How unjust! He was the Messiah. He talked with me here and revealed it. The people heard him speak and were convinced by his words. His death pains me. Did you know him, my lady?"

"I am his mother, woman, and it makes me happy that they believe in him."

"Oh, lady, praise be to God! How fortunate I am to meet you. I was reminded of him when I saw you. May I give you water from my pitcher? It is the same one I gave Jesus."

Refreshed by their rest, they go on. In a day or two they reach sleepy Nazareth. The last rays of sunlight splash across its white dwellings. Talitha opens the door. She is amazed for a moment, then throws herself into Mary's arms with uncontrollable sobs. Everyone is touched to see her pain.

"Enough, Talitha, we have seen Jesus risen. Perhaps you, too, will see him."

The house is clean and in order as always. There is the myrtle tree in the courtyard, the house sparrows chirping on the roof, the chickens waiting for the grains that Mary throws them in greeting. The disciples say good-bye. Stephen stays at Joseph's house. John promises to come back soon from Tiberias.

It grows dark. There is silence. Mary seats herself close to the fire and takes Talitha's hand. Tears fall from her eyes.

Knowing he will not return to this house, she cannot contain the weeping she has restrained for so long. The disciples cannot see her; she can cry freely.

"My God, what has happened? Son, what have they done to you? How they tore your flesh with those lashes and that spear! I cannot forget it. The cross they nailed you to doesn't leave my mind. You preached only goodness and love to all. How much it cost you, son, to love us!

"Talitha, do not be upset at a mother's tears. It will not happen again. Tell me, how have you been?"

"Aunt Mary, may I hug you?"

The rhythm of life in Nazareth is different from what it was. Many relatives, friends, and followers of Jesus come to the house. Although she wants to be alone, Mary receives them, talks to them all, comforts everybody. Stephen watches silently, never tiring of seeing her. He drinks in everything in the house as well and listens to those who knew Jesus as a child.

John returns from the lake. It has been a joyous trip for reasons that he explains buoyantly as soon as he enters the house: "Jesus was with us at the lake! He waited for us on the shore while we pulled in the net full of big fish. How wonderful it was to see them flipping about inside the boat that seemed ready to sink with them all! It was thrilling for us to eat again with Jesus. He lit the fire and spoke as before. We must go out into the world teaching his doctrine. Mother, would you help us?"

"I will always be with you, John."

"Many people of this land want to see Jesus again. Peter and the others pray with them. They wait in hope. In a few days I will go back. Do you want to come, mother?"

"No, John, I will stay. Talitha and some of the others from here wish to go."

One morning they leave, and Mary is alone again. In a few days they return, tired and happy. Talitha tells what happened.

"Mary, Jesus appeared to us; he talked to us beside the lake. There were about five hundred of us. It was marvelous. I could hardly see him for my tears, but I heard him clearly."

John announces they will return to Jerusalem to celebrate Pentecost there.

"I will go with you, John."

"Aunt Mary, will you leave this house? What am I to do without you! Neither this place nor heaven itself can be the same without you."

"I must be with my new children, Talitha. I no longer belong to myself or to these walls, or to this land. My heart has expanded to all who loved Jesus. Do you want to come, Talitha?"

"No, Auntie, I will stay here, tending this house, filled with memories of Jesus."

"God bless you, daughter."

The next afternoon arrogant agents of the Sanhedrin arrive with temple guards. They knock violently. John and James open the door. They warn them not to follow Jesus. Mary approaches.

"What is happening?"

"Do the agitators gather here?"

"I am the mother of Jesus. This is my home. There are no troublemakers here."

They back off, seeing her bearing, so humble yet so ladylike, and leave, uttering threats.

One rainy and chilly dawn, they set off. Mary, wrapped in her shawl, looks slowly around the house that holds so many dear memories. This has been a real home. Joseph's wife, her child in her arms, helps her collect her few belongings. She is sad. Talitha, eyes reddened by tears, readies things for the trip of so many.

"Stay here, Mary, this is your home!"

"No, Talitha, I must be where God wants."

Talitha cries inconsolably when Mary embraces her and says good-bye.

"Courage, daughter, I am not going so far."

Mary of Cleophas, her faithful friend, cheerful as ever, is ready. She is accompanied by her two adolescent sons and her girls—all who want to be Jesus's disciples.

"Enough, Talitha, we have lots of water outside."

They leave. The roads are muddy. Mist hides the sun. The party is numerous and mixed. John, holding the donkey's halter in view of the slipperiness of the path, respects Mary's silence. Sometimes the sun comes out; other times it rains. Then they find what shelter they can under the trees or in villages.

They travel for a day before arriving at Bethel, and the weather worsens. It turns dark. Gusts of wind whip dead leaves into their faces. A flooded stream bars the way. Close by is a small house, with a battered roof and lacking a good door. Here they seek refuge from the rain. Thunder rumbles; lightning flashes across the sky. Mary, at the far end of the shed, sits upon a rickety bench, close to the women. At her feet, on the earthen floor, are Peter, John, and James. Stephen and the others begin to pray against the roaring of the storm. The rain beats down fiercely, while the wind seems bent on tearing off the roof. The river rises, coming dangerously close to the door. The dirty, foaming waters drag logs and branches. This little group—a seed that will bear fruit all over the face of the earth—seems under siege by the forces of evil.

With difficulty they light a torch. Mary's serene visage can be seen in its flickering, and the disciples watch her. "With her among us nothing will happen. She is the mother of Jesus." They pray again. The storm moves away, its din reverberating for a time among the nearby mountains. They settle down to spend an uncomfortable night. A fire dries their clothes, warming faces and food, while their eyes water from the smoke.

Resting against the adobe wall, Mary dozes for a couple of hours among her nieces. Many nights she has slept in such surroundings: before, with Joseph or Jesus, now with these new children whom God has entrusted to her.

At dawn, feeble light filters through the mists rising from the river and ponds. They cross the stream cautiously, John and James on either side of the donkey. When they reach the far shore, the cold waters soak Mary's feet and shawl. But the spring sun warms and dries quickly, and the morning walk becomes easier.

◆ ◆ ◆

Jerusalem is noisy and filled with pilgrims. Every day brings new disciples who congregate in the house where Mary lives, their accustomed meeting place. Lazarus and his sisters arrive; John, son of Mark, receives them with pleasure. He knows them to have been close friends of the Master.

In a few days, while they are gathered in prayer, Jesus appears to them again; speaks to them, teaches them, encourages them, promises the Consoler, and tells them to go next day to the Mount of Olives.

The day dawns beautiful. The air is clear, and high clouds deepen the blue of the sky. The wind carries the scent of orange blossoms from a garden nearby.

The group of early risers departs happily. They will see Jesus again. Mary meditates on this meeting in her heart. Will it not be a good-bye? She goes with them, with a light step, along the almost empty streets of Jerusalem and climbs the slope together with the women. Reaching the top, they wait among ancient olive trees. More disciples arrive; they greet her and talk confidently among themselves. Soon they see Jesus walking toward them from the olive grove. There is silence, and then he speaks. Mary's heart tightens at hearing of his departure. Jesus casts a long look upon them, as though saying good-bye. He takes a few steps back and begins to rise toward heaven. They all watch in astonishment until a cloud hides him; indeed, they keep on looking until angels announce that they will no longer see him. They remain silent; the nieces cry, John lets a few tears drop, and Mary comforts them: "Jesus has said that he will always be with us."

They return, sad at heart that he has left them yet also rejoicing in what they have seen.

Once again they are at Mark's house. More followers are constantly arriving, new disciples, people from places Jesus passed through who have heard that this is where those who love him come together, residents of Jerusalem who watched him pass through its streets bearing the cross, foreigners from neighboring countries who themselves heard the Master, others who did not know him but have heard about him.

At mid-afternoon all go to the temple, Mary and the women separately. When they return, only the apostles, the nieces and nephews, and some women who accompany Mary remain at the house. After a simple dinner, they gather in the cozy upstairs living room; intimacy grows as they recall the last supper with the Master. His mother's presence builds their confidence and fortitude.

They pray, talk, remember the teachings of Jesus. One day, the gathering is special: guided by the Holy Spirit, they elect Matthias to take the place of poor Judas. Mary thinks of his hooded gaze and fawning air. If only he had repented, Jesus would have forgiven him a thousand times, and she herself would have interceded for him.

Matthias—another son. Her heart continues to expand to love them all equally well. John approaches.

"Mother, tell us about Jesus."

"John, my son, I do not like to do it, but today is such a special occasion. . . . I will tell you something that perhaps you aren't aware of. When Jesus was a newborn babe, King Herod of that day, grandfather of the present one, wanted to kill him. Wise Men came from the Orient to adore him. . . ."

They listen attentively as she speaks. The silence is profound. The small oil lamps hanging on the walls are ablaze. Outside the first stars are shining. All of them, together with Mary, have a single love and a single thought.

The days go by. Since the Master's ascension to heaven, fear of the Jews keeps them from meeting at the temple to pray and practice charity. These things they do in the house where many live. Many of the foreign pilgrims still in the city come to the house to learn more about Jesus.

The morning is balmy and warm. Mary sits on a bench set against the lateral wall, with a few women next to her. Peter sits at her right on another bench whose back is to the wall. He is surrounded by the apostles. In front and to her left are the more pious disciples. On the floor, seated on their mantles, are Stephen, the nephews and nieces, and the younger followers.

Sunlight comes through the courtyard window. Outside, friends and followers of Jesus are hoping to be admitted into this community gathered around Mary.

A great sound is heard, as of a strong wind. They fall silent in awe, as do those waiting outside.

Tongues of fire come to rest upon Mary, Peter, and the other apostles. They feel the strength of the divine Spirit penetrating their souls.

The sound ceases, and it is quiet again. They look at each other, surprised, joyful, grateful. Mary feels within her that divine presence she felt more than thirty years ago when she conceived the Son of God.

More people are hurrying to the house, some because they heard the sound, others because they were told of it, all of them astonished and touched. With the others around him, Peter speaks to them from the small terrace. The crowd listens closely. Then Mary and the other women prepare pitchers of water and towels for the baptisms. Mary's heart is filled with happiness: more disciples of Jesus who will go home carrying the good news.

Days pass, and new followers of Jesus continue to arrive. There are so many now that the house can't hold them all. For prayer, they go instead to the temple courtyard. The breaking of the bread is done in smaller groups in people's homes.

One night, Peter and John do not come back from the temple at the usual hour. Mary is uneasy. Several hours go by without news. Then: They are in jail. Anxiety grows. What will happen to them? The people love them, but they also loved John and Jesus. Then more news: They will appear before the Sanhedrin tomorrow. Mary's anxiety is relieved.

Before the day ends, Peter and John return, joyful at having given testimony to Jesus before that body.

These are fruitful times. The church grows. More houses accommodate the newcomers' gatherings. Generosity is practiced among them: they give and are given to.

Dynamic Stephen brings many who desire to meet Mary. From early in the day until evening, Mary is busy receiving people and speaking to them about Jesus. Now she experiences what formerly was said of her son and his disciples: She hardly has time to eat.

John watches her with loving solicitude. The nieces and women of the house care for her with much affection. The sisters from Bethany are quick to serve her in any way they can.

Again her son's disciples are imprisoned—this time it's the apostles. Mary and the women pray for them until late at night, when they return rejoicing, having been freed by an angel.

Early in the morning they all go to the temple to give thanks to the Lord. The Sanhedrin finds out and dispatches guards to seize them without violence. Once again there is continued prayer for them. Hours go by. At mid-afternoon they appear, jubilant at having given testimony to Jesus before the Sanhedrin. Mary and the other women lovingly anoint the wounds inflicted by whips. John has an ugly wound in the neck and lets Mary minister to him.

"John, son, look at what they have done to you!"

"It is nothing, Mother, compared to what they did to Jesus."

Again there is calm among the disciples. Mary and her nieces spend the early part of the afternoon preparing distributions of food, clothing, or money that Stephen gives to the neediest. One afternoon he does not return. Word comes that he has been taken with violence before the Sanhedrin. Hours go by. Mary prays. He is like John: zealous for the things of God. Suddenly there is a commotion and sobbing outside. Mary rushes down and finds Stephen lying on a stretcher and covered in blood. She kneels and holds his head.

"Stephen, my son, your faith in my son has not taken your life from you but given it to you. Now you will be together with him. My God, when will I too be at his side?"

Mary weeps while washing his face and hands. The men who brought him pray; the women weep. All forgive those who have done this.

The first persecution of the disciples of Jesus erupts—unjust like all such persecutions. These people do no harm. Their only offense is following the instructions of the Master in a conse-crated way of life. The apostles remain hidden in various places. They don't gather in Mary's house until night falls. Then there is news about the spreading of the gospel by those who have fled to other parts of Palestine.

One day, judging the city too dangerous, the apostles also leave.

The women are alone, with much work to do attending to the community, the widows, the poor. The persecution that broke out after Stephen's death is forgotten, but not the shed-ding of his blood, the first to be shed for the Risen One.

◆ ◆ ◆

The years go by. The grace of God is tangible. Mary gradually sees the number of her children grow. Her presence is a source of strength, vigor, and comfort for all.

One afternoon there is a timid knock at the door. Mary and Mark's wife receive the visitors: John and Barnabas, and with them a disciple named Paul. At seeing them, Mary exclaims: "John, son, God be praised! How much I hoped you would come back! You are very thin."

John lets himself be affectionately hugged and kissed.

"Mother, God be with you! I have wanted greatly to see you. This is Paul, he to whom Jesus appeared some years ago. He is spreading the gospel among the Gentiles, with great love for the Master."

"How did it happen, Paul?"

"Lady, I was on the road to Damascus. . . ."

Paul tells of his conversion and his apostolate among the Gentiles, his debates with the Jews. Hours go by. Others join them and listen, engrossed, among them, John Mark.

"Paul, I wish to accompany you and Barnabas, to give my life and work for Christ. I will give up what little I have."

"You are welcome to join us. The life we follow isn't easy, but it is rewarding." The day comes to a close. Mary says good-bye to them.

"God be with you, Paul, and bless your work."

More years go by. A growing number of disciples come from distant lands, and John, when he is in Jerusalem, brings them to meet Mary, even if only for a few moments. Mary receives them patiently, trying to understand their languages. To all she breathes courage and hope. Never does she think of herself; when Mary of Cleophas visits from Nazareth, she lovingly rebukes her: "Miriam, you don't have a moment to yourself."

"Mary, what I do is very little compared to the labors of my children, scattered over so many hostile countries, to extend the kingdom of Jesus despite being in constant danger."

One night, trembling and agitated, John announces that Herod has apprehended his brother James and some other disciples. Again they gather in that cozy home to pray for them, keep each other company before this affliction, and be close to the mother of Jesus. As on other occasions, in this atmosphere Mary feels both their great love of God and their fear of those powerful, cruel men, whose vanity leads them to take the lives of their fellow creatures.

The next day comes news that James has been unjustly executed in prison. They are all enormously saddened. Mary lets John recline his head on her bosom and cry.

"Blessed be you, James. You are with Jesus, with John, with Stephen . . . with Joseph."

At dawn they obtain James's body. If only his mother could mourn him! Mary will go to see her if she returns to Galilee. Disciples come and go all morning, anguished at the first death of an apostle. At mid-afternoon they bury him in a small cave near Gethsemane. When they get back, they are alerted that soldiers, preceded by Herodians and temple guards, are approaching. They beat on the door and enter violently. Peter, not protesting, is seized. As he passes Mary, he looks at her confidently. All are frightened—how much blood must this impious king yet shed?

They gather to pray for Peter by the light of the smoking wall lamps. Suddenly there is pounding at the door. Rhoda goes to open it and comes back overjoyed, saying it is Peter. They do not believe her, but she insists. Then Peter enters, pale and smiling. They hug and kiss him, giving thanks to God. He eats while telling what has happened. Hide for a time, he urges Mary and the rest, for there is no telling how far Herod's fury may go. Having said good-bye, he leaves during the night with some disciples. The others gather their belongings and leave stealthily. Mary arranges with the nieces to do so at dawn. She will return to Nazareth after a nine-year absence.

◆ ◆ ◆

Deserted streets, danger at the Damascus Gate. But the armed sentinels let them pass. They are three women in shawls on donkeys—unimportant poor people, the guards think. Thus enters the Queen of Heaven, a humble traveler again on the roads of Palestine.

The trip is tense and hasty. No time for resting or enjoying the scenery. In the early afternoon a squad of soldiers on horseback comes by and hurries on. Has another persecution begun? They won't feel safe until they reach Galilee. Despite their weariness, they hurry faster to get to Nazareth.

Nazareth: life in that rural setting calms spirits: the crowing of roosters, the chirping of sparrows, the tinkling of the sheep bells. The fountain, fresh fruits, the fig tree.

Joseph's girls, Miriam and Ana, are constantly with Mary. Joseph, the oldest son, gazes often at Mary. He resembles his grand-uncle so much! Mary remembers.

"Joseph, Jesus is with you now, he whom you carried in your arms. Jesus, the years soften my memories, but that cross is still there—the cross on which you lay with open arms and your side opened by a lance.

"Joseph, do you believe in Jesus?"

"Yes, Lady Mary."

"Who is Jesus?"

"Jesus is the son of God, our Messiah."

"What does Jesus want from you?"

"That I should love God above all things, my parents, my brothers and sisters, everyone . . . even those fellows that tease me."

One afternoon Mary and her nieces do their spinning together. Someone is at the door. Talitha opens it. With her when she returns is a tired-looking man who speaks with a foreign accent.

"Lady, I am Luke, a doctor from Antioch, a disciple of your son. I have traveled a long way to come here; I am writing about the life of Jesus. Paul, with whom I travel, Peter, and James, told me much about him and his teaching, but nobody has been able to give me information that only you have, my Lady."

Mary observes him thoughtfully. Luke looks with interest at their surroundings.

"How long did he live here?"

"Until the day he left to be baptized by John in the Jordan."

"Was his workshop nearby?"

"Very close, in the house next door. Come, Talitha, let's show him."

They gather up their needlework and take Luke to the workshop, where Joseph greets them modestly.

"Jesus worked here from the time he was a child, first with Joseph, then alone or with cousins. Here is where I used to sit and watch him. Those were years of intense work, which he performed without complaint."

"Lady Mary, how was he born?"

"Come, Luke, let's go into the courtyard. The fig tree is sprouting and turtledoves are nested in the myrtle."

As they come out into the courtyard, a turtledove appears from the shrubs. Mary takes it in her hands with affection.

"Jesus was given a turtledove when he ran after a rabbit as a boy. So many memories! He was born in Bethlehem on a cold night at the end of the year. But I will tell you, Luke, what happened before. It was in the time of Herod, grandfather of this godforsaken king who has just died. My cousin Elizabeth was wife of Zechariah, a priest of the family of Abijah. . . ."

After a time they go back to the house. The nieces have prepared supper in the old kitchen, where the fire heats a big cooking pot from which all serve themselves. Luke is happy. He has been amply repaid for the hardships of his long journey. On finishing their meal, they give thanks to God.

"We will continue tomorrow, Luke. Joseph has a spare room where you can stay. May God be at tip of your pen, as he was with you coming here."

"Thank you, Lady Mary."

The days go by placidly, with the bittersweet taste that recalling days gone by leaves. Events that would not happen again, loved ones who have passed away, places not to be revisited.

James arrives from Judea with some disciples. The persecution is over. They want Mary to return to Jerusalem, for her presence strengthens their faith. She decides to return as soon as the rains end.

Finally the day arrives. The sun shines weakly. Talitha—her eyes red from hidden tears—does not weep. She has resolved not to do so in order not to trouble Mary. Slowly Mary casts a last look around the home. She has a feeling that she will not see it again. Covering her face with her mantle, she mounts the donkey, accompanied by Mary of Cleophas, who says she wants to see her children. Joseph's little one approaches with a basket of cherries.

"Grandma, take them for the journey. Once you start, you won't stop."

"Thank you, daughter. God bless you all, this home, and this land I so love. Good-bye, Talitha, be strong."

The group is numerous. Women ride, men with walking sticks accompany them. James is at the head of the line. Luke asks questions and observes.

Beyond Samaria the heat rises. Summer has begun. Not a leaf stirs. Feeling ill, Mary dismounts and lies down for the rest of the day. James brings her a bouquet of thyme that perfumes the tent; she thanks him with her look, altogether united with God in prayer. Mary of Cleophas and the nieces care for her with tenderness, refreshing her face and hands with damp cloths. The next morning she feels better and can continue the trip.

"James, son, I am no longer up to these trips, on this old donkey. The years weigh heavy."

"We will go slowly, Aunt Mary. There is no rush. When the sun is too hot, we will stop."

They must stop again near Ramah. Mary is pale and breathes with difficulty. The others remain praying around her tent where she rests, a confident prayer to the Son who gave them his mother. Mary calls for James, who approaches with Luke.

"I would very much like to see John. Is he very far away?"

"Yes he is, Auntie, but we will reach him."

The physician Luke kneels beside her, looks into her eyes, and takes her pulse. He prepares an herb drink and has her take it in small sips.

"Thank you, son, though I have no appetite at all, and this is bitter as gall. I will drink it because you asked."

The odor spreads around the tent. At nightfall, Mary falls asleep serenely. The crisis has passed. Luke comes out with tears in his eyes, kneels down on the grass, and, leaning on James, cries with gratitude to God.

Finally they reach Jerusalem, carrying Mary on a rustic stretcher that the men carry with extreme care. Although they are fatigued and the poles hurt their shoulders, none wants to lose his turn. Warned in advance, Mark's mother waits at the door with those of the house. Mary's room is ready to receive her, the bed warmed by a well-wrapped brick, the smell of ripe quinces in the air. The quince was placed in the wardrobe by Mark's mother, remembering something Mary told her Ana used to do when she was a child.

❖ ❖ ❖

Mary recovers. In the afternoons, she again meets in the big living room with an ever-growing number of disciples who want to see and hear her. A few words from her are enough to move them, filling them with faith and boldness to continue on proclaiming Jesus to the ends of the earth.

Luke must leave. Paul is waiting for him impatiently.

"May God bless you, son; write what you have seen and heard. There is more I would have wished to tell you in different circumstances. Take this handkerchief that belonged to Jesus."

Luke falls to his knees and sobs like a child. Mary puts her hand on his head and looks at him with her sweet eyes now shining with tears.

It is hot in the old house, and Mary gets no rest with so many people coming and going. She wears away like those objects of fine gold that become more beautiful the more they are used. Mary's friend and Mark, her husband, discuss the situation with James and decide she should move to a small house on Mount Zion, near Jerusalem. There, peaceful and breathing clear air, she can recover.

Mary leaves very early in the morning so the disciples may not observe her departure. With her are two faithful friends, the nieces, Mark, and James who leads the small donkey.

She takes one last look at the noble old house that generously welcomed her these last years, at the temple, at the Mount of Olives, which evokes so many memories.

The small home is a modest dwelling, but the climate is good. Cicadas hum at noon and birds chirp at nightfall; turtledoves nest in nearby olive trees and cocks crow at dawn.

Mary grows weaker. Consumed by love, she thinks always of Jesus—the loved one—starting long before dawn. She eats without appetite, because she must, takes the medicine they give her, not wanting to disappoint Mark's family's good doctor, who climbs the mountain every day to attend to her. Larks sing below her window, where scarlet geraniums look toward the setting sun.

"James, will John come? I feel that I will be going soon to meet my son. How much I wish to see his face!"

By the middle of the month Mary's condition has worsened. The women do not leave her for an instant. The disciples keep vigil nearby.

"Mary, my good sister-in-law, my childhood playmate, mother of these who are like my own children, I go back to my God. I always sought to be his slave . . . and the slave of his son, my Jesus. What joy to see him soon! I leave you my blue mantle that I brought from Egypt. And to you, my good friend, who welcomed me into your home as one of your own, I leave you my workbasket, which my mother gave me. Give Talitha this ring that Joseph gave me when we married. Distribute my few other things among the nieces who have cared for me. God bless you! I will watch over you from heaven. James, take care of them and everybody else."

The sun seems to set slowly as if to prolong the day and give its last light to the Queen of Heaven. Night falls, a night of shooting stars that drop upon the horizon like tears falling from on high.

The large crowd of disciples that by now has gathered outside the little house is weeping. The whisper of angel wings can be heard around the bed where their queen lies, in a modest bed, between rustic walls, hung with small lamps and bunches of thyme that bring the an aroma of the country into the room.

Mary's white hands rest above the place where once dwelt the son of God. Gathered around her, the apostles and the women pray, weep, and contemplate their dear mother.

At dawn, with the first rays of the sun, Mary exclaims: "Jesus, Jesus, come for me."

She stops breathing and inclines her head. Her face remains serene, utterly beautiful. Unable to withhold their tears, they each approach to kiss her forehead. They bring flowers to place around her bed, the room is filled with aromas and with light from a sun striving to salute the one that has the moon at her feet and wears a crown of twelve stars upon her head.

The morning passes amid comings and goings. So many disciples who loved Jesus venerate his mother. After midday, they take up the most pure body of Mary with great care and carry it on an open bier, covered with flowers, her face barely covered with a veil, to a new sepulcher that Mark's family has in the garden of Gethsemane, a short distance from where Jesus was seized.

The place is spacious and clean. On a great flagstone covered with a linen cloth soaked with aromatic herbs and flowers, they place their precious burden. With another cloth they cover that sacred body, first temple of the Holy Spirit. They leave reluctantly. The last ones to go are the women—no longer tearful. James and two disciples close the sepulcher with a heavy stone slab. Mark seals it with mortar.

Silently they return home and there reluctantly eat a little. There is a sound at the door, and John rushes in, covered with dust, beard grown, dark circles under his eyes, and grief-stricken.

"Mary, my mother, my dear mother! I have not come in time to say good-bye. . . . James, I came as soon as I received your news . . . but tell me how it was."

"It seems as if she were still among us. It was here, in this room, at daybreak. During the trip from Nazareth. . . ." In a steady voice James slowly narrates what happened in the last few days.

Suddenly John says: "I wish to see her, if only for a few moments."

The others are silent. They understand John's wish, although it goes against the customs of their people.

"Let's wait for those who have come from a distance to leave. We will go before nightfall."

The hours pass. John hardly takes a bite. Over and over he asks about those last days of Mary.

In the afternoon the small group goes again to Gethsemane. The slab still closes the entrance. Mark removes the still damp mortar. There is still light from the setting sun that shines among the olive trees on this hillside. They enter the tomb. Mary is not there. The linen cloths that covered her lie folded upon the still fresh flowers and the vials of perfume. All drop to their knees.

"Jesus, your love for her was more powerful than the law of our fallen nature. You took her to you. Mary, now you will be with him in God."

They go out and put the heavy stone back in place. It is sunset. An early star twinkles in the sky as they return to Jerusalem.

One day, many years ago, the heavens joined the earth. On that day the earth joined the heavens. Mary was taken up into that heaven she so often contemplated serenely, searching for the visage of her son who now welcomes her into the glory of the Father.